INDIA'S GLORIOUS SCIENTIFIC TRADITION

Suresh Soni

Ocean Books Pvt. Ltd.

ISO 9001:2015 Publishers

Published by
Ocean Books (P) Ltd.
4/19 Asaf Ali Road,
New Delhi-110 002 (INDIA)
e-mail: info@oceanbooks.in

ISBN 978-81-8430-537-1
INDIA'S GLORIOUS SCIENTIFIC TRADITION
by Shri Suresh Soni

Edition
2026

Paperback Price
₹ 500.00 (Rupees Five Hundred only)

Printed at
Narula Printers, Delhi

INDIA'S GLORIOUS SCIENTIFIC TRADITION

Book by same Author

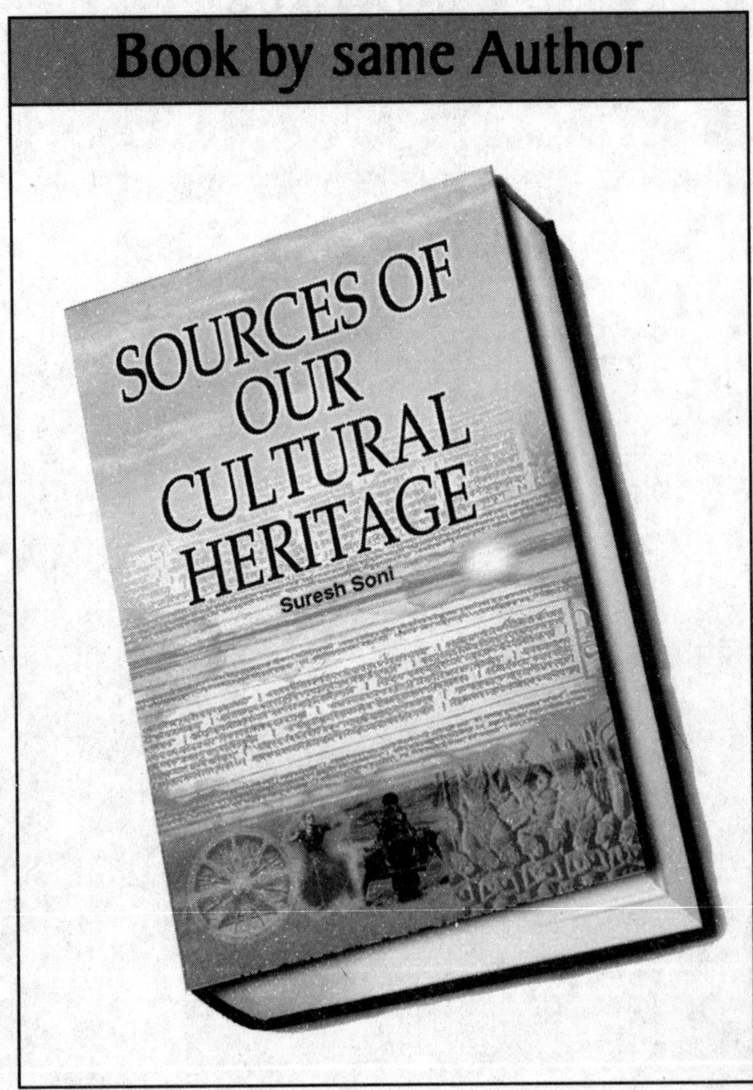

INDIA'S GLORIOUS SCIENTIFIC TRADITION

Author's Note

Most common people feel that the first rays of science broke out in the west and thus, started the wheel of development throughout the world. There was darkness in the field of science in the east. As such, there is a tendency to follow the west. The unawareness of the fact that we had a scientific tradition and a scientific point of view, resulted in the lack of faith that we could have a role in today's world.

However, at the beginning of the 20th century itself, Acharya Prafulla Chandra Rai, Brajendra Nath Seel, Jagdish Chandra Basu, Rao Saheb Vaze, etc., to name a few intellectuals, proved through their studies that India was in the forefront, not only in the field of religious philosophies, but also in the field of science and technology. Not just this, our ancestors had harmonised science and spirituality. It was through this that because of our scientific vision, science developed in accordance with and for the welfare of mankind and entire living beings in general. The modern world is feeling the significance of it today.

Many scholars have, with more proof, written about ancient Indian science in various articles and books. Prafulla Chandra Rai's *Hindu Chemistry,* Brajendra Nath Seel's *The Positive Science of Ancient Hindus,* Rao Saheb Vaze's *Hindi*

Surgical Science and Dharmapalji's *Indian Science and Technology in the 18th Century,* have revealed the traditions of science and technology in India. In recent times, Sanskrit Bharati has carried this forward by publishing many books in Sanskrit on science including botany, physics, metallurgy, machines, chemistry, etc. Besides this, M.P. Rao of Bangalore has carried out experiments in Aero-science and P.G. Dongre of Varanasi also carried out some experiments. The Vigyan Bharati, Mumbai and Pathey Kan, Jaipur tried to present to society the collected form of all the above efforts. The writings and speeches of Dr. Murli Manohar Joshi have impressively portrayed the ancient tradition of Indian science.

Besides, through the speeches and experiences of Friedzov Kapro, Grezukov, Jyofrieschve and esteemed Swami Ranganathanandaji and Swami Jitatmaanandaji of the Rama Krishna Mission about the coordination and the harmony between science and spiritual contemplation, which is the most important need of today, Indian scientific thought and its speciality is being revealed to the world. Many scholars are carrying out contemplations and experiments in this direction. Today's generation can get a direction from reading this literature; they can gain self-respect and can save the world from many problems which it is experiencing because of only materialistic development.

On the basis of the books and articles written by these scholars, I had given two speeches on the glorious tradition of science in India. Urged by my friends, I have expanded those two speeches and written them in the form of this book.

However, I do not consider myself to be the author of this book because whatever I have written here, all the facts and proofs that I have given, were given by various scholars in their books, speeches and articles. Hence, my role, at the most, has been that of a compiler. Whatever is written here is the creation, of those I have mentioned at the end of this book in the reference or glossary. I express my heartfelt gratitude to all those scholars.

Shri Sudarshanji (himself, a telecommunication engineer) who is the head of the Rashtriya Swayamsewak Sangh, read this book, corrected the mistakes in the language and suggested measures to make it more useful. I am therefore, obliged to him.

Smt. Purnima Majumdar translated my Hindi book into English, I entend my heartfelt gratitude towards her.

My friend Shri Arun Ojha from Patna read the book from beginning to end and with considerable effort, removed many linguistic errors because of which the book turned out to be even more useful. I am therefore grateful to him.

Dr. K.P. Joshi, Professor in Physics from Devi Ahilya University made some suggestions to clarify certain aspects, while Shri Jayant Gopal Ranade from Sangli made suggestions to include some references. Dr. Sadanand Damodar Sapre, Professor in the Electronics Department of Maulana Azad National Institute of Technology, Bhopal, once again read the book and gave suggestions for improvement.

Many friends advised that it would be proper to give the reference of the shlokas and facts mentioned in the book. Hence, chapter-wise references have been given at the end of the book.

I hope that besides acquainting the modern generation with India's contributions in the field of science, it will also inspire them to study more and experiment. If this is possible even in a small measure, I shall consider my effort worth its while.

—Suresh Soni

Contents

1

India: Past and Present

THE GLORIOUS PAST

There are many countries in the world. If we go deep into history, we realise that for ages, India has been the source of inspiration for humanity. Our ancient ancestors transmitted the feeling of "***Krinvanto Vishvam Aryam***"- we shall make the entire world excellent; "***Vasudhaiv Kutumbakam***" – the entire world is one large family and "***Swadesho Bhuvantrayam***"- all three worlds (Bhoomi, Swarg and Paataal) are our own native land. Besides this, they also contributed arts, skill and philosophy for happiness and worldwide prosperity. It is for this reason that India was called the 'Preceptor of the Universe' (Jagatguru) in ancient times. One can see reflections of it in the writings of the western philosopher, Mark Twain. He says, "India is the land of religious orders, the cradle of humanity, the birthplace of languages, mother of history, grandmother of the *Puranas* and the great grandmother of tradition. Whatever valuable and creative things are there in the history of man, all are available in India. Everyone is eager to get a glimpse of this land and they will not be ready to sacrifice it for all other things of this world."

India was not just the leader in dharma, philosophy, metaphysical knowledge and human values, but also in trade, commerce, art and skill.

A famous Swiss writer, Bajoran Landstram who had studied everything from the ancient Egyptians to the stories about the various travels and the great explorers till the discovery of America, wrote in his book, *The Discovery of India,* "There were many paths and means, but only one goal—to reach the famous land of India, which is full to the brim with gold, silver, valuable stones and gems, tempting foods, spices and clothes."[1] Many thinkers and researchers like Hegel, Galileo and Marco Polo have similar experiences as those of Bajoran Landstram. That is why India has been called 'The Golden Bird' for ages.

The country remained the *Jagatguru* and 'The Golden Bird' for years. The continuous barbaric invasions on it for 1500 years, some social flaws, the relentless attacks of the Muslims and the economic exploitation by the British in the 190 years rule, made the Golden Bird bankrupt. Indian agriculture, industry and trade were ruined. That is why, today, we find India at 124th position in the countries of the world.

Today's generation is faced with the challenge of reviving India's position as the Golden Bird and the *Jagatguru*. The freedom fighters' and thinkers' dream of a glorious India is to be fulfilled by the present generation.

For this, it is essential that progress be made in the arts, skill, trade, commerce, agriculture, etc. Principally, the world still recognises India's superiority in the fields of Dharma and philosophy. However, when the question of physical prosperity or a society whose behaviour is in accordance with the philosophy arises, it becomes difficult to reply. Hence, it is necessary to contemplate on the hypothesis of all-round progress and its methods.

Thousands of years ago, *Maharishi* Kanad, had, while speaking about all-round progress, said, "***Yatobhyudayanih shreyas siddhihi sa dharmah***" – the medium through which one acquires all kinds of development – from the physical point of view and the philosophical point of view, is called Dharma.

Unfortunately, during the past, our country has been making efforts from the spiritual point of view, but in the context of all-round progress, physical progress was neglected, whereas physical progress is not only essential for all-round progress, it is even considered compulsory.

When the question of physical progress in society is considered and we think of its medium or device, we realise that they have been changing in the flow of time. For instance, agriculture, cow protection and commerce were the medium of our physical prosperity at one time. This is to say that cow protection and trade were the basis of agriculture which was the basis of the prosperity on the family and social levels. In fact, they remained the medium of our prosperity for thousands of years. Indian agriculture and prosperous business were recognised around the world, as it spread all over the world. Even if we leave the description of ancient times and consider India's condition on the issue of production in 1750, then in the comparative chart given in Samuel Huntington's book, *The Clash of Civilisations* clarifies that India's production was more than that of Europe and the Soviet Union. (This included the Soviet Union before it broke up and all the countries in the Warsaw Pact.) India's production was 24.5 per cent, while Europe's was 18.2 per cent and that of the Soviet Union was 5 per cent.[2]

THE SIGNIFICANCE OF SCIENCE

Change comes with time. Once, agriculture and trade were the standards of prosperity. But today, with scientific development, a change seems to have come about in the means of production. Today, science and technology have become the media for the invention of the tools of physical prosperity, production and distribution. Today, the country with developed science and latest technology will speedily march ahead.

In this context, if we want our country to once again be at the helm of affairs and the top of prosperity, and be able to contribute something to the world, we need to give a boost, not only to our scientific and technological development, but also remember that this development is not contrary to our culture, nature and need. In order to achieve both, we shall have to consider many points:

1. Are science and technology a gift of the west only or did India also have a tradition of its own?
2. In which spheres had science been developed in India?
3. Was there any scientific knowledge in India about the final purpose of science and technology? And if there was any, what was special about it?
4. Does Indian science vision have any solution to the various problems the world is facing, with regard to the development of science and technology?

THE FACTS TODAY

When we consider the first question to find out about the history of science in India, we are faced with today's ground reality. We can understand it from two to three incidents narrated below:

1. An organisation named Sanskrit Bharati has been functioning for the last few years to publicise and

propagate Sanskrit and make it a mass-language. In order to educate people about the fact that Sanskrit is not just a language of religious philosophy, but also of science and technology, it has prepared five frescos or mural paintings. These have been prepared to tell people how the references of mathematics, physics, chemistry and astronomy, available in the ancient Sanskrit scriptures, have a semblance to the modern scientific discoveries and inventions. With the intention of publicising this fact, Mr. C.M. Krishna Shastri, the national organising secretary of the Sanskrit Bharati went with the five murals in February 2001, to talk to the senior officials of the Ministry of Science and Technology of the Government of India. In the murals on mathematics, the officials saw that centuries ago, Aryabhatta had calculated the value of pi as 3.1416. They were surprised and exclaimed, "Wow! Our ancestors had calculated the value so many years ago!" This incident indicates that those who decide the direction of the development of science in India, are so ignorant about the knowledge of scientific tradition in India.

2. The other is a slightly older incident. The earlier Shankaracharya of Puri, Bharti Krishna Teerthaji had, through his *sadhana* and meditation, discovered some amazing mathematical formulae and sub-formulae in the background of *Shulbhasootras* and the Vedas. With the help of these 16 main and 13 sub-formulae, all types of mathematical problems and equations can be solved very easily. On the basis of these formulae, he wrote a book called *Vedic Mathematics*. Keeping the importance of this book in mind, some people went to the Tata Institute for Fundamental

Research, and requested the head there, that this was a remarkable contribution in the field of mathematics and to test it out and keep it in their library. But the institute did not accept the book, saying that they did not have any belief in it. The book that was rejected, became the issue of debates and discussions, when a foreign mathematician, Nicholas came to Mumbai from England and told the mathematicians about the uses of the formulae and called it 'magic'. This was highlighted and publicised by the *Times of India*. This incident tells us that if a foreigner had not told us their importance, our mentality would have been not to accept it.

3. The third incident - The former Human Resource Development and Science & Technology Minister, Dr. Murli Manohar Joshi became a member of the Uttar Pradesh Curriculum Committee in 1962. During this exercise, he realised that the Pythagoras Theorem, perhaps one of the most feared amongst students, had been solved before Pythagoras by Bodhayan in India. While Pythogoras' method was long, tedious, complicated and boring, Bodhayan's was very short and simple. Hence, he told the other members of the Curriculum Committee about this and requested that it should be called the Bodhayan Theorem, so that on the one hand the students would get a simple theorem, on the other hand, knowing that this was a contribution of our country, it would increase their self-confidence. However, the Curriculum Committee did not agree. He kept trying to convince them. Another fact came to his notice during his efforts. Edward Taylor, a renowned physicist, associated with the discovery of the hydrogen and atom bombs, and a nobel laureate,

had written a book called *Simplicity and Science*. In the book, he argued that the study of science should not be complicated, obscure or boring, instead it should be simple, accessible and enjoyable. From this point of view, he gave the Bodhayan Theorem as an example of how simple the solutions can be, to mathematical problems. When Dr. Joshi told the Committee members about this example of Edward Taylor, they said that since he was so keen and had been requesting so many times, the theorem could be renamed the Pythogoras – Bodhayan Theorem.[3]

The above incidents tell us that generally, in society, there is no belief that there was a scientific tradition in India. Another thing worth noticing is that if there is any discussion with any student of any level (primary or graduate or post graduate or research scholar) and they are asked whether they have read anything in the context of India's contribution in the field that they are studying, be it politics or economics or science, the answer is usually in the negative. In the same manner, from an ordinary student to prominent people in the country, there is a lack of knowledge about the existence of a scientific tradition and its originator in this country.

THE REASONS FOR OBLIVION

Lord Thomas Babington Macaulay had implemented the British system of education so that future generations do not feel any pride in their tradition, culture and history. Gradually, with the end of Sanskrit schools, English schools became compulsory. In the curriculum that was decided for these schools, no mention of any contribution by India in any field, especially in the field of science, was allowed in the textbooks. As a result, in the course of time, the degree holders that graduated from these schools, were bereft of any information of India's contributions. This was their colonial agenda; therefore the British tried to cut education from our roots. Yet, it was believed that after independence, India's traditional contribution would be included in the education in order to arouse self-confidence. However, unfortunately, even after independence, the same curriculum continued, which showed Europe as the main contributor to scientific tradition. As a result, ancient India's discoveries, works and results could not become a part of the education which has been continuing for the past 170 years. Studying this curriculum which is disconnected from Indianness, has had an ill-effect on the Indian psyche. It was believed that any contribution in the world from the point of view of development has been given by Europe. Therefore, a feeling of pride that we also have contributed something, is missing and has been replaced by one of an imitator and a slave like mentality.

THE CONSEQUENCES OF OBLIVION

In order to realise the absence of self-confidence about ourselves, two experiences of the present President and renowned scientist, Dr. Abdul Kalam will be helpful. There is a dream of a self-reliant and developed India in his eyes. This he has expressed in his book *India Two Thousand Twenty: A Vision for the New Millennium*. In this book, while the path to a developed India has been laid down, he has also mentioned the biggest hurdle in this path, through two of his experiences.

On the first incident, he writes, "There is a multicoloured calendar hanging in my room. This beautiful calendar has been printed in Germany and it has pictures of Europe and Africa taken by satellites. Whoever sees these pictures gets very inspired. However, when the person is told that these pictures have been taken by an Indian

Telesensing Satellite, his face shows disbelief and it doesn't quieten down till he reads the credit given at the bottom of the calendar to the Indian Satellite for the pictures."

About the second incident he writes, "Once I was invited to a dinner where there were many scientists from abroad as well as many important people from India. Discussions moved gradually to rocket technology. Someone said that the Chinese had discovered explosives thousands of years ago. It was later, in the 13th century that with the help of this gunpowder, fire arrows began to be used in wars. Participating in this discussion, I enumerated one of my experiences, when I had gone to England sometime ago to a place called Woolich near London, which has a museum called Rotunda. In this museum, I saw the rockets used by Tipu's armies in the battle with the British in Sri Rangapatnam and these were the first rockets in the world to be used in a battle. On my saying this, one prominent Indian immediately retorted that the technology for this had been provided to Tipu by the French. At this, I very humbly told him that he was not saying the correct thing. I told him that I would give him the proof. After some time I told him about the book called *The Origins and International Economics of Space Exploration,* written by Sir Bernard Lowell, in which he says that William Congrave had studied the rockets used by Tipu's army, made some improvements and in 1805 presented them before the then British Prime Minister William Pitt and Secretary of Law Kraiser Leed. They were impressed and consented to include them in the army and used them in 1806 in the battle with Napoleon near the Boulogne harbour and in 1807 in the attack on Copenhagen. After reading the underlined portions in the book with great concentration, this prominent personality said that it was interesting. He found it interesting, but there was no feeling of pride towards this great Indian discovery.

Unfortunately we have forgotten some of the best creative people of our country. The Britishers keep all the information about Congrave, but we know nothing about the great engineers who designed the rockets for Tipu's army. The reason for this is the foreign influence and feeling of inferiority that the intelligent people of our country suffer from, and this is the greatest hurdle for the country."[4]

Owing to the above mentioned defeatist psyche, we are not able to inculcate the belief that we have our own traditions of scientific and technological developments. With our brilliance, we can make new inventions and make a place for ourselves amongst the developed countries. In fact, not just this, we can make our own contributions too. As a result, the picture that we have drawn of our country is one that believes that we shall develop only with the help of western technology and wealth. Hence, we are neck deep in debt and look up to the foreign countries for their technology. If we want to change this picture, we shall have to rid ourselves of this inferiority complex. No one can become great by depending on others. In his convocational address at the Science College of Prayag in 1949 Sir C.V. Raman told the students, "Boys, when we import, we not only pay for our ignorance, but we also pay for our incompetence."[5] Every single person in the country needs to consider what he had said.

Along with this, the speech of the famous scientist, Acharya P.C. Roy on Hindu Chemistry in Madras in 1918, is worthy of consideration in order to arouse self-respect. In the speech he had called for pride about the country's contribution. His words were – "We are not ashamed of our ancient contributions to the science of chemistry. I am equally proud of and not ashamed of all the branches of science that grew in ancient India."[6]

In order to change our present psyche, about ourselves,

our traditions and our capabilities, we shall have to contemplate on some fundamental aspects.

To begin with, we have a notion that a person from the west is intellectual, logical and a believer in experiments, whereas an Indian considers only books to be the proof, is with blind faith and tends to run away from experiments. But, what is the reality? Let us glance at Western and Indian history.

□

2

Views of the West and India Towards Logic and Experiments

VIEW OF THE WEST ON LOGIC AND EXPERIMENTS

Experimental science seems to have made its appearance in the west about 450 years ago with Galileo. Before that, Copernicus had established the scientific belief that the sun is stationary and the earth goes around it. However, when we analyse the ideologies and the psyche of society, we realise that Aristotle was a pervasive presence regarding any answer to any question on life. There was a tendency among the people to try to find out what Aristotle had said regarding any issue for which a solution was found to be difficult. There is an interesting anecdote in this connection. A few scholars were once discussing something in a hall in London. The topic was how many teeth did a horse have? Each scholar stated a different number. So, they could not come to any conclusion - a youth was sitting beside and listening the discussion eagerly. Suddenly, one scholar said, "For the final decision, let us see what Aristotle has said." So, one scholar went to a nearby library, to look for a book by Aristotle. The youth who had heard this, went out of the hall, without attracting anyone's attention. However, when after sometime, he returned, everyone stared at him, because he had brought a live horse with him. Presenting the horse before the scholars, he said, "Why trouble Aristotle? The horse is here. Count its teeth and decide."[1]

Before Galileo, everyone the world over believed that a heavy object will fall faster than a lighter one, because Aristotle had said that a ten pound stone would fall ten times faster than a one pound stone. Galileo challenged this belief and said that if we neglect the air resistance, then both the objects will fall together on the ground. The moment Galileo proposed this belief; the entire city pounced on him and asked whether he considered himself more intelligent than Aristotle. Galileo said that he could prove his theory, thereby arousing everyone's curiosity. Hence, the entire town collected near the Tower of Pisa on the day Galileo had said he would prove his theory, through an experiment. As the people watched in anxiety, Galileo climbed the tower and threw down a one pound and a ten pound stone together. The spell bound people saw that both the stones fell down together. Those who saw this happen said that Galileo definitely knew 'black magic' as Aristotle could never be wrong. Such was their belief in Aristotle. This incident shows what kind of a psyche people of Europe had around 450 years ago.

The British consider themselves very intelligent, but they had never seen cotton fibre until they came to India. Hence, the cotton plant, the cotton fibres, the thread made of it, and the cloth were all new for them. All they knew was that wool was taken from sheep and cloth made from it. Hence, they used to say that Indians were very clever. They grow the wool on plants that ought to be on the sheep and weave cloth with it.[2] These facts speak volumes about the European mentality and their views on experimentation.

It is true that Europe has made unmatched progress in the fields of science and technology in the last 150 years, but what was their society like, before that? If we glance at how one, who said anything against the Bible or the Church was treated, we'll get to know about the European mentality.

1. Till about 1500 years before the birth of Galileo, Aristotle's beliefs and ideologies ruled over Europe. In 139 AD, Claudius Ptolemy, inspired by Aristotle, established the idea of an earth-centric world, according to which, the earth was at the centre and the sun moved around it. This was patronised by the Church. Hence, these beliefs dominated the entire western world for centuries. In 1543, Copernicus, who was born in Poland, refuted Ptolemy's belief and established that the sun is at the centre and the earth goes around it. This was the starting point of history of western science. But Copernicus died before this theory, which was opposed to the Church, was published. However, when it was published later, it was banned.
2. Galileo invented the telescope and examined the sky with it. He found that the Copernicus theory that the sun was at the centre, was right. At this, the people who believed in Ptolemy, considered the use of the telescope sacrilegious. In fact, religious leaders said that it was against the holy scriptures to consider Copernicus correct. They compelled him to apologise and vow that he would never do any such work in future as it was against religion. He was kept under

house arrest. He wrote a book on physics, but even before it was published, he became blind and in 1642, at the age of 78 years, he died while still under house arrest.

3. Copernicus' principle that the sun is in the centre was, in 1546, supported by Taiko Bruno, who was an astronomer and born in Denmark. An expert in mathematics and metallurgy, Bruno recognised 750 stars without the help of a telescope. He established that there are many other worlds like the earth. Incensed by his arguments, the Pope and the clergymen kept him in prison for eight years. Since he did not compromise and refused to apologise, he was burnt to death in 1600 AD.
4. John Kepler, a German born in 1571 was an associate of Bruno. He made a deep study of astronomy and found out the rules about the position and the movement of the planets and prepared maps of their orbits. His understanding was considered against religion. The Catholics attacked him. He kept running away and in a state of poverty and sickness, he died a tragic death in 1630.

These incidents; which tell us of the way in which the people who tried to establish their own theories or who went against theories already set, were burnt alive, arrested and compelled to die, show the attitude the west had until about 400 years ago on logic and experimentation.

INDIA'S VIEW ON LOGIC AND EXPERIMENTS

For thousands of years, we, in India, have had complete freedom in education. No one was arrested or burnt alive because of his thoughts. Let us take an example. In India, we have always had sacred feelings towards the *Vedas*—

the treasure of knowledge and their seers. About them and those who created them, the materialist Charvak has said, ***"Trayovedasy kartaarah bhandadhoortanishaacharaaha."*** That is, those who created the three *Veda*s are hypocritical, cunning and evil. Despite such distorted statements, Charvak was never ill treated. In fact, he was also accorded the status of a philosopher.

Let us see another example. In the *Mundakopanishad,* it is written that Shaunak, the head of a big *gurukul* went to Sage Angira and asked him that the knowledge of which element amounted to knowing everything? In reply, Sage Angira said, "There are two elements—one is the metaphysical, which gives us the knowledge of the ultimate (*Para Vidya*) and the second is the physical, which gives us worldly and heavenly happiness (*Apara Vidya*). However, comparatively speaking, metaphysical learning is better than physical learning." Explaining physical learning, Sage Angira said, "The *Veda* and its subordinate branches are *Apara Vidya,* i.e. physical knowledge; still the society continued to honour him."

For thousands of years, blind faith or proof of scriptures did not have the last say in India. Instead, logic and actual experience had recognition. Hence, in his lectures on *Gita,* Adi Shankaracharya has said, "If hundreds of *Shrutis* (*Shrutis* of *Upanishads* are considered beyond logic as they are born out of solid experiences) say that fire is cool and a non-illuminator, they cannot be considered as evidence because it is in opposition to actual experience." (*Gita Adhyaya 18, Shloka 66* - Shankar Bhashya).

To know what India's view on experiments was, one must note portions of Dr. Murli Manohar Joshi's speech at the golden jubilee session of the Indian Parliament—

1. "Today, we are told to look westwards for any scientific discovery. What is happening in the US

and Germany, or in Japan or France? However, 200-250 years ago, circumstances were absolutely the opposite and 1000-1200-1500 years ago, things were even more reverse. Before I mention India's ancient scientific traditions, I would like to say that what is told to us is really an illusion. We are told that experimental sciences were born in the west; that the west taught the world to experiment, that before that there was no experimental science and if there was any scientist in India, he was merely a theoretician, who had invented the zero, the infinite. That Bhaskaracharya brought out some mathematical formulae and that experimental sciences came from the west. All this is nothing, but an illusion. Famous Indian scientist Acharya P.C. Ray says—

"When the Royal Society, an important institution in the field of science, was established in 1662, philosophical experimentarians like Hobbes, Locke, etc. used to make fun of its founders Boyle, Hooke and Christopher and for hours, people used to discuss whether a dead fish was heavier or a live one."

On the other hand, Acharya Ray gives an example of what the conditions were like in India. There are two books related to Hindu chemistry. One is *Rasendra Chintamani* and the second one is *Rasprakash Sudhakar.* These were written respectively by Rasayan Shastri (chemists), Ramchandra and Yashodhar, who were born in the 13th century. In this Ramchandra says, "Whatever I have heard from scholars and read in the *Shastras,* but have not proved myself, have not been included in this book. On the contrary, I have written only what I have proved by experimenting, with my own hands under the able guidance of my teachers."

Furthermore, Ramchandra says that a real teacher is one who can, through experiment, prove what he has taught and a scholar is one who can prove it again. Those who can do so are real teachers and pupils; the rest are like characters in a play.[3]

Yashodhar, who was also born in the 13th century, has expressed the same concept in his book, *Rasprakash Sudhakar* –

Swahasten Kritam Samyak Jaaranam N Shrutam Maya.
Swahasten Bhavayogen Kritam Samyak Shruten Hi.
Dhanubandhstritiyoasau Swahasten Krito Maya.
Drisht Pratyay Yogoayam Kathitona Ch Sanshayah.[4]

(Rasprakash Sudhakar)

"I have not just heard of *Jaaṛan* (causing decay, condiment, a digester, oxidising of metals), but have also done so with my own hands on the basis of the knowledge that I have heard of earlier. On the basis of that, I proved the creation of the third metal myself."

2. All the musical instruments that were made here are examples of experimental science. These were not mere elemental or theoretical analyses, but were born out of examination, inspection and experimentation. Musical instruments are the saga of the analysis and the use of the creation of sound; its various forms and effects. *Natyashastra,* written by Sage Bharat, is an example of how it was created by experimenting. In the 33rd chapter of this epic, its author Muni Bharat gives a description of how the *mridanga* and the other instruments came into existence. A sage named Swati lived in a *gurukul* in

ancient times. There was a holiday in the *gurukul* and scarcity of water. So, Sage Swati went out in search of water. He reached a water body where lots of lotuses were blooming. Their leaves were spread over the water in the pond. Suddenly, it became cloudy and, after a strong breeze, it started raining heavily. The water started flowing all over the land. A beautiful sound was heard when the water fell on the leaves. Sage Swati was amazed to hear the beautiful sound that was created by water falling on lotus leaves. When examined, he realised that the leaves were of different sizes—some big, some medium and some small. Because they were of different sizes, even the sound of water falling on them was varied. A deep sound was heard from big leaves, a soothing sweet sound from the medium ones and a touching, sentimental sound from small leaves. He merged with the scene and the sound; and in deep thought and feeling, returned to the *ashram* with the big, medium and the small leaves and started experimenting as to how he could create the same sound. At first, he experimented with water, then with other means. In this process, musical instruments like the *mridanga*, the *panav* and the *dardur muraj*, etc. were created.

These examples tell us that we in India always valued reasoning and proof more than blind faith. We have had the freedom of thoughts and experiments since those times, when the west could not imagine it even in a dream. Hence, acquainting and familiarising our present generation with the scientific tradition of our country will be a medium to free the country from its inferiority complex and develop the feeling of self-sufficiency and self-respect. □

3

Western and Indian Concepts of Science

Let us briefly consider three questions from the Western and Indian points of view – (i) What does science mean? (ii) How far does the boundary of science extend, or what is the extent of science? (iii) How is science expressed?

THE WESTERN POINT OF VIEW

1. In his book, *Grammar of Science,* Carl Pearson interprets the work of science as "a division of facts, their arrangement and their comparative significance. To draw a conclusion while remaining impersonal from personal experiences is the characteristic feature of a scientific approach."[1] Hence, we can say that science becomes active through a sequence of enquiry, experiment, investigation, reasoning or analysis and conclusion.
2. In the context of the extent or boundary of science, the *Encyclopedia Britannica* says, "the Latin word ***Scientia*** means knowledge. In the present times, it

is used in the context of such knowledge, whose extent is so vast, that no individual can understand more than one part of it. The knowledge related to science is varied. This difference extends from the atoms to mental functions...from the birth and death of constellations to the migration of birds...from the minutest creatures to gigantic nebulas (milky way), from the rise and fall of granular or crystalline particles to the creation and disintegration of the universe. The knowledge of actions and the rules of thoughts of living beings, and of the hurdles are also included in this."[2]

3. Two forms of science have been acknowledged - one is pure science and the other is practical science (applied science). The ultimate truth of the universe and the search for the rules governing it are included in pure science. And practical science includes understanding these rules and the inventions to make human society's standard of living more and more comfortable and convenient. From the point of view of applied science, a number of sciences developed in the west – physics, chemistry, biology, metallurgy, astronomy, mathematics and their numerous branches.

THE INDIAN POINT OF VIEW

1. In the tenth chapter of his treatise of Indian philosophy, *Vaisheshik* India's first nuclear scientist, Sage Kanaad says, "***Drishtanaam Drishta Prayojananam Drishtabhave Prayogoabhyudyaye***" – that is, the path to prosperity is led by experiments seen by oneself, carried out to show to others, or to go deeper to gain more knowledge.

   Similarly, in order to find out from an ordinary

particle to the universe and their importance, Sage Gautam talks about a 16-stage process in his *Nyaya Darshan*. *Pramey* (theorem/probandum) means "that which has to be known". *Praman* (proof) means the tools which are used in order to know. *Sanshay* (doubt) is that for which the investigation is done. To know the different parts of the ultimate solution is known as *avyaya* (components). After that, the hypothesis is placed. Then, with the help of various examples and cases, efforts are made to reach the truth. This is how the process has been laid down.

2. The Indian version of the process of knowing is clearer. It has been said that the world where we work, the visible world as well as its entire business and the reason for the existence of the universe, both have to be known. Today, the west is observing the world, but they do not know much about the observer.

   In the seventh chapter of the *Gita*, Lord Krishna says that in order to know the holistic form of Brahma, we must know the knowledge and science, for then we need not know more. He adds that we must know about the one who is on land, that is, solid; water, that is liquid; and air, that is gas; fire, that is energy; sky, mind, intellect, ego, that are the supreme element, we must know about all this.

   In the same way, Sage Kanaad says that one must know the land, water, brilliance, air, sky, direction, mind and spirit. It includes all living and non-living things of the entire world and nature.

3. The ultimate purpose of knowledge and science is to find the reason of the world. From this point of view, many of the references have been mentioned in the *Vedas*, *Upanishads* and the philosophical

treatises. This includes the creation of the universe, its sequence, the rhythm and the rules that govern creation. Besides, from the point of applied sciences, physics, chemistry, botany, agriculture, mathematics, astrology, biology, ayurveda, metallurgy and the various artistic skills were also fields of study and experiment. The context is visible in Narad's conversation with Sanat Kumar in the first part of the seventh chapter of *Chhandogyopanishad*. Narad once went to Sanat Kumar and pleaded for knowledge. At this Sanat Kumar asked, "What have you read? What do you know?" (chha. 7/1/1) in reply, Narad said, "Lord, I have read *Rigveda, Yajurveda, Atharvaveda, Samaveda,* history, the Puranas—the fifth *Veda,* grammar, maths, astrology, jurisprudence, logistics, ethics, theology, demonology, astrology, music, dance, sculpting. I know the *mantras,* but not spiritualism, for one who is spiritual can go across the sea of sorrows. Hence, give me that knowledge." (chha 7/1/2, 3)

In the following pages, we shall try to find out India's tradition and contributions in the various fields of pure sciences and applied sciences.

When we read ancient Indian scriptures, like the *Vedas, Upanishads, Brahman, Aranyak, Puranas, Mahabharata, Ramayana,* etc., some incidents described therein, give us an inkling of scientific development - incidents like Ashwani Kumar regenerating Upamanyu's vision in the *Upanishads,* Anusuya reviving Shandili's husband after his death. Ashwani Kumar freeing Sage Chyavan of his senility. When we read about Ravana having control over various physical powers, the three cities of Tripurasur would move on earth, sky and in water, Arjun's war with the demons of Paulumi, a celestial town, and the space crafts of the various Gods, the description of the divine arms, the *Pushpak* aircraft which could fly at wish, we get a picture of a developed civilisation. Then the question arises whether these are mere stories, fables or poetic imagination because if it did happen, then what was its technique? Are there some scriptures on this technique? The biggest hurdle in finding this out is the fact that everything is in Sanskrit and most of the manuscripts are lying scattered at random. There are, however, some scriptures which are proof of the progress in applied science. We can find out about these from them.

SCIENTIFIC TRADITION

From the scientific point of view, there has been a tradition of study and research since ancient times. A number of sages like Bhrigu, Vashishtha, Bharadwaj, Attri, Garg, Shaunak, Shukra, Narad, Chakrayan, Dhundinath, Nandeesh, Kashyap, Agastya, Parshuram, Drona, etc. who spent their entire lives on working in the fields of aeronautics, astrology, chemistry, military science, ship building and all other walks of life.

For example, in defining architecture, what Bhrigu has written encompasses such a vast periphery of knowledge, that it is difficult to imagine.

Nanavidhanam Vaastunam Yantranam Kalpasampada.
Dhatnnam Sudhananam Cha Vaastnnam Shilp-sangyitam|
Krishirjalam Khanishcheti Dhatukhandam Tridha-bhidham.||
Nauka-Rathagniyananam, Kritisadhanamuchyate|
Veshm, Prakar, Nagarrachana Vaastu Sanggitam||

– *(Bhrigu Samhita-1)*[3]

Bhrigu mentions ten *shastras* – agriculture, hydrology, mining, shipping, charioteering, rocket science, Weshm

Shaastra (House building, palace, temple, public place and fort's building), Praakaar Shaastra, town planning and mechanical engineering, etc. Besides these, there is a mention of 32 different types of learning and 64 types of arts. These include metallurgy, textiles, health, agriculture, building dams, forestry, war science, bridge building, printing, boating, charioteering, air crafts, town planning, house building, health, zoology, botany, cooking, entertainment, administration, etc. Seeing the list of subjects, it seems that the periphery encompassed the entire life. There were many scriptures about these sciences, many of which have been lost and many have disappeared with the people who knew them because we have always believed that knowledge should not fall into the hands of unrightful people. Although it is true that a lot of knowledge has been lost, yet, even today, several manuscripts are lying scattered around. What is required is to study, analyse and use them. This process may probably reveal new areas of knowledge. In this book, we shall discuss some aspects of Indian scientific uses, tradition and development in the ancient and modern times. We shall first discuss it from the point of view of applied sciences.

□

4

Electrical Science

Rao Saheb Krishnaji Vajhe had passed the engineering exam in 1891 from Pune. While looking for scriptures related to science, he found a few pages of the *Agastya Samhita* with Damodar Tryambak Joshi of Ujjain. These belonged to around *Shaka Samvat* 1550. Later on, after reading the said description in the pages of the *Samhita,* Dr. M.C. Sahastrabuddhe, the Head of the Sanskrit Department in Nagpur felt that the description was very similar to that of Daniel Cell. So he gave it to P.P. Hole, the Professor of Engineering at Nagpur, with a request to investigate. Agastya's sources were as follows:

> ***Sansthapya Mrinmaye Patre Tamrapatram Susanskritam***
> ***Chhadyechhikhigriven Chardrarbhih Kashthpamsubhih.***
> ***Dastaloshto Nidhatavyah Pardachhaditastah***
> ***Sanyogajjayte Tejo Mitravarunsangyitam.***
>
> — (*Agastya Samhita*)[1]

"Take an earthen pot, place a copper sheet, and put the *shikhigreeva* in it. Then, smear it with wet sawdust, mercury and zinc. Then, if you join the wires, it will give rise to *Mitravarunashakti*."

When Mr. Hole and his friend started preparing the apparatus on the basis of the above description, they could understand all the things except *shikhigreeva*. On checking the Sanskrit dictionary, they understood that it meant the neck of a peacock. So, he and his friend went to Maharaj Bagh and asked the chief when a peacock would die in his zoo. This angered the gentleman. Then they told him that they needed its neck for an experiment. The gentleman asked them to give in an application. Later, when during a conversation, they narrated this to an *Ayurveda* expert, he burst out laughing and said that here it did not mean the neck of a peacock, but a substance of that colour, that is copper sulphate. This solved the problem. Thus, a cell was formed and measured with a digital multimeter. It had an open circuit voltage of 1.38 volts and short circuit current of 23 milli amperes.

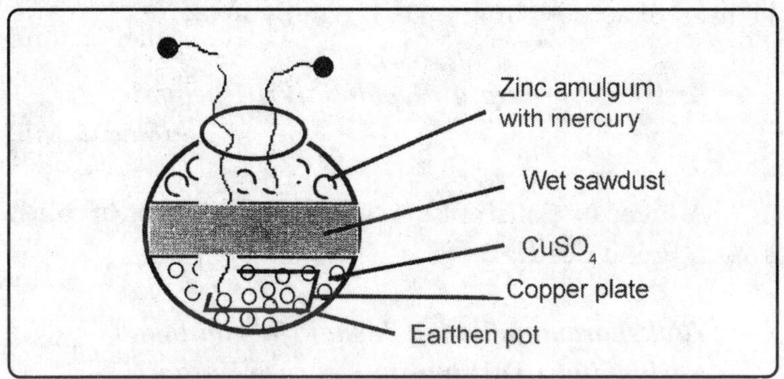

The cell, according to the description of *Agastya Samhita*

The information that the experiment was successful was conveyed to Dr. M.C. Sahastryabuddhe. This cell was exhibited on August 7, 1990 before the scholars of the fourth general meeting at the Swadeshi Vigyan Sanshodhan

Sanstha, Nagpur. It was then realised that the description was of the electric cell. They investigated as to what the context was and it was realised that Sage Agastya had said many things before this.

Anen Jalbhangosti Prano Daneshu Vayushu
Evam Shatanam Kumbhanamsanyogkaryakritsmritah.

— (*Agastya Samhita*)[2]

He says that if we use the power of 100 earthen pots on water, then water will change its form into life-giving oxygen and floating hydrogen.

Vayubandhakvastren Nibaddho Yanmastake
Udanah Swalaghutve Bibhartyakashayanakam.

— (*Agastya Samhita- Shilp Shastra*) [3]

If hydrogen is contained in an air tight cloth, it can be used in aerodynamics, i.e. it will fly in air.

Kritrimswarnarajatalepah Satkritiruchyate

— (*Shukra Niti*)

A layer or polish of artificial gold or silver is called *satkriti* (good deed).

Yavksharamyodhanau Sushaktjalsannidhau.
Aachhadyati Tattamram Swarnen Rajten Va
Suvarnliptam Tattamram Shatkumbhmiti Smritam.

– (*Agastya Samhita*)[4]

In an iron vessel and in a strong acidic medium, gold or silver nitrate covers copper with a layer of gold or silver. The copper that is covered by gold is called *shatakumbha* or artificial gold.

Rao Saheb Vajhe, who spent his life in rummaging the Indian scientific scriptures, and discovering various experiments, gave different names to electricity on the basis of the *Agastya Samhita* and other scriptures and that electricity is created in different ways.

1. Lightning - created by friction of silken cloth
2. *Saudamini* - created from friction of gems
3. Electricity - created by clouds
4. *Shatakumbhi* - created by 100 cells or pots
5. *Hridani* - stored or assimilated electricity
6. *Ashani* - born of magnetic bar.[5]

Agastya Samhita also contains an account of how electricity can be used for electroplating. He also discovered a way to polish gold, silver, and copper with a battery. Hence, Agastya is also called one who is 'Battery Born'.

□

5

Mechanics (Kinetics) and Mechanical Science

In *Vaisheshik Darshan* by Sage Kanaad, it is mentioned that (work) or action means motion. There are five kinds of motion:

1. *Utpekshan* (Upward motion)
2. *Avkshepan* (Downward motion)
3. *Aakunchan* (Motion due to the release of tensile stress)
4. *Prasaran* (Shearing motion)
5. *Gaman* (General motion)

It has also analysed the different motions on the basis of reason:

1. because of propulsion - continuous pressure.
2. because of effort - such as moving of the hands.
3. because of the gravity - just as something falls down.
4. because of fluidity or liquidity - with the impact or influence of minute particles.

In his book, *The Physics,* Dr. N.G. Dongre compares the velocity mentioned in the vast commentary written in the 1st century in *Prashastpad Bhashya* to Newton's Laws of Motion (1675).

Prashastpad writes,

> ***Vego Panchasu Dravyeshu Nimit–Visheshapekshat Karmano Jayate Niyatdik Kriya Prabandh Hetuh Sparshvad Dravyasanyog Vishesh Virodhi Kvachit Karan Gun Purv Kramenotpadyate.***

"Motion is caused by five substances or matter and is created by special objects. It gets created and destroyed also by actions done in the regular direction."

The above mentioned commentary of *Prashastipad* can be divided into three parts, and then we can find the striking similarity with Newton's Laws of Motion.

1. **Vegah Nimittvisheshat Karmano Jayate**
   The change of motion is due to impressed force. (*Principia*)

2. **Vegah Nimittapekshat Karmano Jayate Niyatdik Kriya Prabandh Hetuh**
   The change of motion is proportional to the motive force impressed and is made in the direction of the right line in which the force is impressed. (*Principia*)

3. **Vegah Sanyogvisheshvirodhi**
   To every action there is always an equal and opposite reaction. (*Principia*)[1]

Here, the definition of *Vaisheshik* is given along with Newton's Laws of Motion, that velocity or force is a physical entity created by motion or work.

ELASTIC FORCES

Elasticity is the name given to the property because of which rods, plates, etc. vibrate and emit sound. *Vaisheshik* Philosophers knew this. It is mentioned in Udayan's *Nyay Karikavli*.

Stithisthapaksanskarah Kshitah Kvachichchturshvapi
Ateendriyosau Vigyeyah Kvachit Spandepi Karanam. – 59

In the other kinds of matter, solid or liquid the invisible force created in the substance is the cause of the vibration.[2]

In Bhaskaracharya's book, *Siddhant Shiromani* (written in the 12th century) in *Shlokas* 53-56, of the mechanics of the *Goladhyaya,* the water wheel has been described.[3]

Tamradimayasyamkushrupanalasyambupurnasya. – 53
Ek Kudajalantardvitiyamagram Tvadhomukham Ch Bahih
Yugapanmukt Chet K Nalen Kundabdahih Patati. – 54
Nemyam Baddhva Ghatikashchakram Jalayantravat Tatha Dharyam
Nalakprachyutsalilam Patati Yatha Tadghati Madhye. – 55
Bhramati Tatastat Satatam Purnghateebhih Samakrishtam
Chakrachyutam Tadudakam Kunde Yati Pranalikaya. – 56

That is, if one takes a copper rod, folds it like an elephant driver's hook and dips one end in a vessel of water and leaves the other end face downwards outside, then all the water of the vessel will flow out of the tap. Tie the vessels and place them in a circle. Place the two ends of the axis in such a way that the water that falls from the tap, falls into the vessel. This way, the circle will go on continuously and the water that falls from the circle, falls into the reservoir through the drain.

Analysing the book *Samarangan Sutradhar*, edited by

Bhoj in 1150 AD, Rao Saheb K.V. Vajhe's information about the machine in 1926, conveys the impression of a developed mechanical knowledge. From the point of view of all machines, something has been said about some basic or fundamental things.

> ***Prakritya Parthivam Sthiram Shesheshu Sahja Gatih***
> ***Atah Prayen Sa Janya Kshitavev Prayatnatah.***
>
> – (*Samarangan*-31 *Sutradhar*)

The earth is naturally stationary. All machines, with respect to this static earth, are forms of motion produced in matter by artificial means.

THE MEANS AND WORKS OF MACHINES

The main means of the machines have been described in the book, *Yantrarnav*.

> ***Dandaishrchakraishrch Dantaishrch Sarnibhramanadibhih***
> ***Shakterutpadanam Kim Va Chalanam Yantramuchyate.***
>
> – (*Yantrarnav*)[4]

Yantra or machine is a contrivance consisting of...

Dand – Lever
Chakra – Pulley
Dant – Toothed wheel or gear
Sarani – Inclined plane
Bhraman – Screw

and is required for producing *shakti* (power or motion) or change in direction.

Their main works are- Stirring
Centralising motion
Stopping
Bringing together
Annihilation.

Each machine has three parts—

1. *Beej* - The producer of the action, i.e. motor.
2. *Keelak* - The pin joining power and work i.e. greel.
3. *Shakti* - The ability of doing work, i.e. power.

Thus, a machine moves because of its three parts; five means and the activities that they do. These together create a variety of movements.

Tiryagurdhvamadhah Prishthe Puratah Parshvayorpi
Gamanam Saranam Pat Iti Bhedhah Kriyodbhavah.

—(*Samarangan ch-31*)[5]

Various works require a number of movements to do the work.

1. *Tiryag* – Slanting
2. *Oordhva* – Upwards
3. *Adhah* – Downwards
4. *Prishthe* – Backwards
5. *Puratah* – Forwards
6. *Parshvayoh* – Sideways

What qualities a machine must have are described in the *Samarangan Sutradhar*, speaking of the twenty qualities like the interrelationship of the parts, of how one does not have to take special care while it works, how to use less power that it should not make much sound, parts must not become loose, there should not be much variation in speed, time management should be taken care of, so that it works for a long time, etc. Later, it has been mentioned in the book—

Chirkalsahatvam Ch Yantrasyaite Mahagunah Smritah.

—(*Samarangan ch-3*)

Longativity is a major quality of a machine.

Hydraulic machine (turbine)—In the 31st chapter of

Samarangan Sutradhar, with reference to the use of water current in the generation of power, it has been said—

> ***Dhara Ch Jalbharashch Payso Bhramanam Tatha.***
> ***Yathochchhrayo Yathadhikyam Yatha Neeramdhratapi Ch***
> ***Evamadeeni Bhujasya Jaljani Prachakshate.***

"The mass and momentum of flowing water current is used in hydraulic machines or turbines for the generation of power. Water current rotates an object and if the water falls from a great height, it has greater impact and the turbine moves in proportion to its weight and speed. This generates electricity."

> ***Sangriheetshch Dattashch Pooritah Pratinoditah***
> ***Marud Beejatvmayati Yantreshu Jaljanmasu.***
>
> —(*Samarangan-31*)[6]

"Collecting water, allowing it to flow and reusing it is a path to use force as power. This process has been described in greater detail in this chapter only. We also get some other references about mechanical science."

During the reign of the Chalukyas, they had a self-operational system of draining water from a tank in the garden. This is described in the journal of Anantacharya Indological Institute, Bombay.[7]

The *Viman Shastra,* written by Sage Bharadwaj has the description of a number of machines with which we shall deal in the context of the chapter on Aeronautics.

The 31st chapter of the *Samarangan Sutradhar* of Raja Bhoj is an authority in mechanical science. This chapter gives a description of many machines like wooden airplanes, mechanical soldiers and watchmen; one may also catch a glimpse of a robot in it.

□

6

Metallurgy

Since ancient times, metallurgy has been used in day to day life in India. It is mentioned in the *Yajurveda* –

> ***Ashma Ch Mai Mrittika Ch Mai Giryashch Mai Parvatashch Mai Siktashch Mai Vanaspatayashch Mai Hiranyam Ch Maiyashch Mai Shyamam Ch Mai loham Ch Mai Sees Ch Mai Trapu Ch Mai Yagyen Kalpantam.***
>
> – *(Kr. Yaju. h-7-5)*

"May our stones, mud, mountains, sand, vegetation, gold, iron, copper, lead and tin grow with *Yajna.*"

In the *Ramayana,* the *Mahabharata,* the *Puranas,* and the *Shrutis* also metals like gold, iron, tin, silver, lead, copper, bronze, etc. have been mentioned.

Names of some people engaged in different fields of metallurgy:

Karmara	–	One who melts raw metals
Dhamatra	–	One who blows the fire in the oven
Hiranyak	–	One who melts gold
Khanak	–	Miner[1]

Ancient Indian physicians like Charak, Sushruta and Nagarjuna have described in detail how to prepare medicines from gold, silver, copper, iron, mica, mercury, etc. One does not find a mention of developed metallurgy in ancient scriptures alone; but evidence is available even today. Some are as follows:

1. **Zinc –** The discovery of zinc is an amazing thing in the field of metallurgy. The process of refining zinc through the distillation process is a matter of pride for Indians. Excavations in the Jawar region of Rajasthan, have revealed a process of zinc making dating back to the 4th century BC. With only 10 per cent zinc, brass starts shining like gold. Chemical analysis of the brass items found in the Jawar region of Rajasthan showed that it had more than 34 per cent of zinc, whereas, according to the known methods of today, under normal circumstances, not more than 28 per cent of zinc can be added to brass.

   Melting zinc is also a complicated process because under normal pressure, it starts boiling at 913°C. To procure pure zinc from zinc oxide or from raw zinc requires a temperature of 1200°C, but at that high temperature, zinc turns to vapour. Hence, in those days, to oxidise zinc, the raw zinc had to be roasted, then it was heated by adding coal and salt in calculated quantities and placed in earthen pots at a temperature of 1200°C. At this temperature it vaporises, but Indians had developed a process called reverse distillation. Proof of this has been found in the excavations at Jawar. Oxidised vessels of zinc were heated in an inverted position, in an atmosphere of carbon monoxide. As soon as the zinc vaporised, it was taken to a cool place below, where it took on the metal form. This way, pure zinc could be obtained. This knowledge of acquiring zinc was prevalent in India much before the birth of Christ.

Until 1735, Europeans believed that zinc could not be obtained in element form. In Europe, William Champion was the first to get the process of refining zinc patented as the Bristol Process. This he had copied from India because it is exactly like the process mentioned in the 13th century book, *Rasratnasamuchchay*.[2]

2. **Iron**—One finds references to the good quality of Indian steel in history. People in Arabia and Persia were very eager to get swords made of Indian steel. The English named the steel with highest carbon content as 'Butz'.

   Famous metallurgist, Professor Anantaraman of the Banaras Hindu University, has explained the entire procedure of making steel. Raw iron, wood and carbon are heated in earthen bowls at a temperature of 1535°C and then, slowly cooled over 24 hours. This gives high quality carbon rich steel. A sword made of this steel is so sharp and strong that it even cuts silk smoothly.

   In the 18th century, some European metallurgists tried to manufacture Indian steel, but failed. Even Michael Faraday tried, but was unsuccessful. Some succeeded in manufacturing it, but the product wasn't of good quality.

   Shri Dharmapal has, in his book, *Indian Science and Technology in the 18th Century,* mentioned the proofs that the western world has cited about an advanced iron industry in India. In September 1795, Dr. Benjamin Hayen sent a report to the East India

Company, in which he talks of Ramnath Peth (a small, beautiful hamlet in the then Madras Presidency) and says that it is a beautiful village. There are mines and forty furnaces for steel. The steel thus manufactured costs Rs. 2/- per *mana* (32 kilograms). Hence, the company must contemplate along these lines.[3]

The second report was sent by Major James Franklin, in which he wrote about the production of steel in central India. He described the iron mines at various places like Jabalpur, Panna, Sagar, etc. He says that charcoal is used all over India to manufacture iron. The furnace, he mentions, were constructed. All its parts were of an average of 19-20 cubit (1 cubit ≈ 18 inches) and a small furnace size was 16 cubits. He describes the procedure of making this furnace. When he measured the entire furnace, he found out that the measurement was the same—its length, 4¼ parts; width, 3 parts; thickness, 1½ parts. He further writes that parts like the (1) *guradiya* (2) *pachar* (3) *garery* or puley and (4) *akariya* were used. Later, when the furnace was completely dry, it was used for working. After the furnace, he describes the blow, its nozzle and the process of refining the iron. He then examined the process of manufacturing steel and its proportions from April 30, 1827 to June 6, 1827. During this period, 223½ *mana* (31¼ *mana* = 1 English ton) of steel was made from four furnaces and he has openly and warmly praised the speciality, quality and grade in various temperatures and circumstances.[4]

At that time, one *mana* of steel cost only 11¾ annas.[5]

Quoting Presgrave, the Captain of Sagarmint,

Major James Franklin says that the iron bars of India were of a superior quality. It even outdid the Swedish iron, which was considered the best in Europe at that time.

The third report is of 1842 by Captain J. Campbell. It describes the production of iron in south India. All these reports state that at that time, there were thousands of small steel manufacturing furnaces. About nine people could get employment with one furnace and good quality and cheap iron was produced.[6] That was not possible in any other country of the world. While looking for bar iron for the railways, Campbell said that India's bar iron was not just of high quality, but also cheap. Even the best iron in England could not compete with India's low quality iron. At that time, 90,000 people were employed with these furnaces. In 1874, the British established the Bengal Iron Company and started large-scale production. Costly steel was imported from abroad. As a result the consumption of steel produced in the villages began to decline and by the end of the 19th century indigenous steel manufacturing virtually stopped. Starting large factories, the British virtually broke the backbone of indigenous technology. The sad part is that Indian metal technology nearly vanished. Today only a few examples of this technology remain with a few tribal people of Jharkhand.

THE IRON PILLAR IN DELHI – A MIRACLE

The iron pillar next to the Qutab Minar in Delhi has been the centre of attraction for metallurgists from all over the world. For nearly 1600 years, it has been standing undaunted under the open skies, during all types of weather conditions. In so many years, it has not rusted; this has been a matter of surprise for the world.

As far as the question of its history is concerned, it was made in the 4th century. According to the Sanskrit inscription on it, it was set up as a flag post in front of the temple of Lord Vishnu on the Vishnu mountain in Mathura by Chandra Raj. It may have been made to place Garuda on top of it. That is why it is also called the Garuda pillar. It was brought to Delhi in 1050 by Anang Pal, the founder of Delhi.[7]

The pillar is 735.5 cms tall, of which 50 cms is below the earth and 45 cms is in the stone platform around it. It has a circumference of 41.6 cms at the base, and 30.4 cms above. It might once have a statue of Garuda on top of it. The total weight of the pillar is 6096 kg. A chemical examination in 1961 showed that the pillar is made of surprisingly good quality steel and contains much less carbon in comparison to the steel of today. Dr. B.B. Lal, the chief chemist of Indian Archaeological Survey has concluded that the pillar is made by joining 20-30 kgs of hot iron pieces. It is believed to have been manufactured in 15 days by 120 workers. The fact that 1600 years ago the technique of joining pieces of hot iron, was known to us, is a matter of amazement by itself because not a single joint can be seen in the whole pillar. The fact that despite remaining in the open, and weathering it out for 16 centuries, it has not rusted, has amazed expert scientists. It has more of phosphorous and less of sulphur and manganese. Large quantities of slug by itself or collectively increases resistance to rust. Besides this, a 50-600 micron (1 micron = 1000th part of 1 mm) thick layer of oxide also protects the pillar from rusting.

3. **Mercury**—Until the 17th century, the Europeans did not know what mercury was. Hence, in documents

of the French Government, it was called quick silver—another kind of silver because it shone and could move from one place to another. The government also made a law that those Indian medicines which contained mercury, could be used only by specialists.

In India, people not only knew about mercury, they were using it on a large-scale in pharmaceuticals also for thousands of years. Al Baruni was the first foreigner who stayed for a long time in India in the 11th century. He had, written in detail, in his book, about how to manufacture mercury and how to use it, and acquainted the world with it. We shall discuss how to purify mercury when we discuss chemistry, but it is believed that Nagarjuna, who was born in 1000 AD, knew how to make gold with mercury. What is surprising is that he chose mercury, and not any other metal, to convert it into gold. Modern science says that a metal is produced on the basis of the number of protons in an atom of a metal and it is amazing that while there are 80 protons and electrons in Mercury, in gold there are 79 protons and electrons.

4. **Gold-Silver**—A. Delmar, in his book *A History of Precious Metals* - 1902, New York, says that there are two islands named Chryse and Agyre at the origin of the River Sindhu, where particles of gold and silver can be found in the soil of the entire land.

The 7th *mantra* of the 61st *sookta* of the 6th division of the *Rigveda* names the Saraswati and Sindhu (Indus) as *Hiranyavartani*, that is gold.

Gold and silver are mentioned in the scriptures like *Ramayana, Mahabharata, Srimad Bhagwat Gita,*

Raghuvansh, Kumar Sambhava, etc. The tradition of using gold ash, for medicinal purposes has been prevalent in India for centuries.

Similarly, we find references of the use of gold, copper and lead in the *Atharvaveda, Rasa Tarangini, Rasayan saar, Shukra Neeti, Aashwalayan grihyasootra,* and *Manusmriti.* In the *Rasaratnsamuchhay Granth,* the process of making the ash of many metals and using them to cure various diseases, is given in detail. This shows that metallurgy had developed in India in ancient times and used in various ways for the welfare of man.

KERALA'S *DHATU DARPAN*

When Dr. Murli Manohar Joshi went to a place called *Aaranmuda,* in Pattanam Titta district of Kerala, he found that the families there knew the technique of preparing mirrors from metal by hand. When he showed these to his friends in the science committee, they could not believe that they could have been made by hand and not by machine, and that for ages, they were being exported from India. We never tell our students that such a technique is present in India, and despite the fact that these people live in poverty, they are not prepared to leave it for fear that this traditional art might vanish. The country must take care of such people. □

7

Aeronautics

It is generally believed today that man's dream of flying like birds was fulfilled when the Wright Brothers made the aeroplane on December 17, 1903 and that aeronautics is the west's gift to the world. There is no doubt that this knowledge has made tremendous progress but during the Mahabharata period, and even before that, it had been developed in India too. Not just aeroplanes, cities too had been created in space. A number of references to this have been found in the Indian texts. In explaining the meaning, of the 1st *mantra* of the 36th *sookta* of the *Rigveda*, Vidyavachaspati Pandit Madhusudan Saraswati in his book, *Indra Vijay* says that the Ribhus had made a three-wheeled chariot, which could fly in space. In the Puranas, the various Gods and Goddesses, the Yakshas, etc. travelled by air. The Tripurasur, that is the three demon brothers had constructed three invincible cities in space. They could commute between earth, water and sky. They were destroyed by Shiva. The *Ramayana* has reference to the *Pushpak Viman*. In the *Mahabharata*, the plains of Sri Krishna and Jaraasandh are mentioned. Bhagwat also refers to Sage Kardam, who, because of his penance, could not pay attention to his wife. When he realised it, he took her in his aircraft and showed her the entire universe.

When today's experimenting and logical person reads or hears this, he naturally thinks that they are all fantasies and imaginations to entertain human beings. It is natural to get such thoughts because no books or ancients remnants have been found to prove the fact that these planes were present in ancient times and that people knew the technique of building them.

Fortunately, at least one book is available, which tells us that in ancient times, people in India had knowledge about planes and it was quite developed. This book, its contents, and its descriptions, have been attracting the attention of scholars in our own country and abroad for years.

During a discussion in the context of the status of science in ancient India, Shri Subodhji, an industrialist from Delhi narrated an experience. His younger brother works in NASA in the USA. One day, in 1973, he rang up to say that one of his American scientist friends who was also working in NASA, wanted a treatise by Sage Bharadwaj on Aeronautics. Subodhji was surprised because this was the first time he had heard about this book. Later, after great effort, he procured it from Mysore and sent it to USA.

In the *Hindu Culture* edition of *Kalyan* published from Gorakhpur in 1950, Sh. Damodarji 'Sahityachar' mentioned this treatise in his article 'Hamari Prachin Vaigyanik Kala' in detail. Sh. Prahalad Rao, a retired engineer from the Air Force in Bangalore became curious and with the assistance of the Aeronautical Society of India and his friends, began a project—'Aeronautical Science Rediscovered'. On the basis of extensive study and his own experience, he proved that this book contained the description of a very developed aeronautical science. Sh. M.K. Kawadkar of Nagpur has also done a lot of work on it.

Sage Bharadwaj had authored a book called *Yantra Sarvaswa*. One part of it is on aeronautical science (*Vaimanik Shastra*). Bodhanand had written a commentary on it. *Yantra Sarvaswa* is not available today and even *Vaimanik Shastra* is not completely available. However, whatever is available is enough to make us believe that planes were indeed a reality in the past.

The first chapter of *Vaimanik Shastra* has a list of 25 books on ancient science. The prominent ones are *Shaktisutra* authored by Agastya, *Saudamini Kala* authored by Ishwar, Anshubodhini, *Yantra Sarvaswa* and *Aakash Shastra* authored by Bharadwaj, *Vayutatva Prakaran* authored by Shaka Tayana and Vaishvanarantra, *Dhoom Prakaran* etc.—authored by Narad.

Bodhanand, who has written the commentary on *Viman Shastra*, writes:

Nirmathya Tadvedam Buddhim, Bharadvajo Maha Munih;
Navnitam Samudghritya, Yantrasarvaswarupakam.
Prayacchat Sarvalokanamipsitarthphalapradam;
Tasmin Chatvarinshatikadhikare Sampradarshitam.
Nanavimanavaichitriyarachnakrambodhakam;
Ashtadhayayrvibhajitam Shatadhikarnairyutam.
Sutraih Panchshatairyuktam Vyomyanpradhanakam;
Vaimanikadhikaranmuktam Bhagwata swayam.

He says that by churning the ocean of the *Vedas*, Sage Bharadwaj brought out the butter named *Yantra Sarraswa* which would bring forth the desired fruit for humanity. The 40th chapter mentions aeronautics, which tells us the sequence of building an airplane. This book is divided into 8 chapters, 100 charts and 500 formulae and the airplane is the main subject.

After telling us about the book, Sage Bharadwaj writes about the scholars of aeronautics before him and their works. They are[1] –

1. Narayan – Viman Chandrika
2. Shaunaka – Vyomayaan Tantra
3. Garg – Yantrakalpa
4. Vachaspati – Yaan Bindu
5. Chakrayani – Khetyaan Pradeepika
6. Dhundinath – Vyomyanark Prakash

In this book, Sage Bharadwaj has defined an airplane, the pilot whom he calls a mysterious official, the path in the sky, the clothes, parts of the plane, power, machine and the various metals required to build it have also been described.

DEFINITION OF A PLANE

Narayan Rishi says, a plane is one that can move fast like the birds on the earth, water and sky.

According to Shaunaka, it is one that can go from one place to another *via* the sky. According to Vishwambhar, a plane is one that can go from one country to another and from one planet to another.[2]

PILOT

Sage Bharadwaj says that one who knows the secrets or mysteries of the aircraft only, can be the rightful flier. The *shastras* speak of 32 secrets to fly a plane. One who is aware of all the varieties can only be a successful pilot because it is impossible to fly a plane unless one has the knowledge of how to make a plane, take it from land into the sky, to land it, moving it forward, moving it in a zigzag motion or hovering and to change its velocity. Hence, one who knows these secrets is the mysterious authority and, therefore, has the right to fly a plane. Some of the prominent secrets are:[3]

3. ***Kritak Rahasya***—This is the 3rd of the 32 secrets. According to this, manufacturing planes as desired, from the essential metals on the basis of the *viman shastras* of Vishwakarma, Chhayapurush, Manu and the Maydaanav, is given. In a way, we can say, it is a description of the hardware.
5. ***Goodh Rahasya***—This is the 5th secret and tells us how to hide the plane. According to it, if, through the powers of the wind, one can attract the power of darkness in the sun's rays, and can establish a relationship with the aircraft, then, one can hide the aircraft. As per the chapter on the elements of wind, the *yasa, viyasa and prayasa* which are present in the 8th circumference of *vatsambha* can be used far above purpose.
9. ***Aparoksh Rahasya***—This is the 9th secret. According to this, if the *rohini* electricity mentioned in the *Shakti Mantra* is spread, then everything that comes in front of the aircraft can be seen clearly.
10. ***Sankocha***—This is the 10th secret. According to this, one can reduce the size of the aircraft as required, while flying.
11. ***Vistrita***—This is the 11th secret. According to this, when required, the size of the aircraft can be increased. It must be noted here that in the present time, this technique has been developed after 1970.
22. ***Sarpaagaman Rahasya***—This is the 22nd secret according to which, it is possible to fly the plane in a zigzag path, like a snake. It is said that by tunnelling

the seven kinds of air and the power of the sun rays to the nose of the aircraft, and then pulling it into the blowpipe that produces power, one can make the plane fly in a zigzag path.

25. ***Parashabd Grahak Rahasya*** – This is the 25th secret. It says that according to the *Saudamini Kala Granth,* if you place the *shabd grahak yantra* on the plane, one can hear what people on the other plane are talking.
26. ***Roopakarshan Rahasya*** – With this one can look into another plane.
28. ***Dikpradarshan Rahasya*** – With the machine called *Disha Sampatti,* one can find out the direction of the other plane.
31. ***Stabdhak Rahasya*** – By throwing a special gas called *apasmar* into another plane by the *stabdhak yantra,* one can make everyone in the other plane unconscious.
32. ***Karshan Rahasya*** – This is the 32nd secret. According to this, if one finds an enemy plane attacking one's plane, one can light a fire in one's *vaishwanar* channel and heat it till it reaches 87 *links* (a measure of temperature like degree celsius). Then pushing the buttons of both the pillars, one can spread that power around the enemy plane in a circular manner so as to destroy it.

AIRWAY

Sage Shaunaka divides the airways in *five* different ways while Dhundinath speaks about the different whirlpools on the heights of various paths and then gives an indication of hundreds of paths on each of those heights. He gives a detailed description of the powers working there and the paths on various heights upto 100 kms above the earth.

The description of the airways and their whirlpools is as follows:[4]

10 km (1)	-	Whirlpool of energy
50 km (2)	-	Wind
60 km (3)	-	Solar rays
80 km (4)	-	Cold current
90 km (5)	-	Collision

FOOD OF THE AVIATOR[5]

It gives a description of the kind of food suitable for a specific season. The airplanes at that time were a little different from the planes of today. Today, we have airports for the planes to land. At that time, they could land anywhere. Hence, if during a war, they had to land in a forest, then how would the aviators survive? For this, a description of 100 vegetables on which an individual could survive for 2-3 months is given.

Another significant thing that has been said in the *Vaimanik Shastra* is that a pilot should not fly a plane on an empty stomach. In this context, Mr. M.P. Rao of Bangalore says that when pilots of the Indian Air Force would fly fighter planes in the mornings, they would sometimes meet with an accident. An analysis showed that the pilots were flying on an empty stomach. Hence, in 1981, a system of giving breakfast to the pilots started in the Indian Air Force.

THE MECHANISMS IN A PLANE[6]

The *Viman Shastra* talks of 31 kinds of machines and their specific places in the plane. The functions of these machines is also described. Description of a few machines is as follows:

1. ***Vishwa kriya darpan***—With this instrument, the pilot could see the activities going on outside from within the plane. Mica, mercury etc. were used to make it.

2. ***Parivesh kriya yantra*** – This describes the auto pilot system.
3. ***Shabdaakarshan yantra*** – This helped one to hear sounds within a 26 km area and the plane could be saved from accidents by hearing the sounds of birds.
4. ***Guha garbha yantra*** – This helped in finding explosives under the earth.
5. ***Shaktyakarshan yantra*** – This helped in attracting the poisonous rays and converting them into heat and releasing it into the atmosphere.
6. ***Dishadarshi yantra*** – Used to show the direction.
7. ***Vakra prasaaran yantra*** – Made it possible to turn back the plane immediately if an enemy plane appeared in front suddenly.
8. ***Apasmaar yantra*** – Could emit poisonous gas at the time of war.
9. ***Tamogarbha yantrao*** – With this, it was possible to hide the plane during war and *tamogarbha* iron was the main component in its manufacture.

SOURCES OF ENERGY

Sage Bharadwaj mentions four kinds of energy sources needed to fly an aeroplane:

1. **Vegetable oil** which works like petrol.
2. **Mercury vapour** - There is mention of its use in the form of energy in the ancient scriptures. The US experimented with it in flying aeroplanes. However, when it went up, it exploded. But it proved that mercury vapour could be used as a source of energy. There is a need for more flawless experimentation.
3. **Solar energy** - Aeroplanes could fly with this as well.
4. **Atmospheric energy** - Without any other means, flying the aircraft by using energy taken directly from

the atmosphere, like the boat moves when you open the sails, due to the power of the wind. In the same manner, the aircraft in the sky would keep moving by absorbing energy from the atmosphere. Efforts in this direction are on in America. This description shows how extensively scientists in ancient India had thought about the various sources of energy or power.

TYPES OF AIRCRAFTS[7]

Sages of aeronautics have mentioned aircrafts according to the age and the times. The *mantrika* types, which had a mixture of the physical and the mental powers, were possible in the *Satyug* and the *Tretayug*. It has reference to 25 kinds of planes. The *tantrika* types of aeroplanes were there in the *Dwaparyug*. There were about 56 types of tantrika. In *Kaliyug,* the *kritika* type of machine-driven planes had been described and about 25 types were operational. The important ones in this were *Shakun, Rukm, Hunsa, Pushkar, Tripur,* etc.

On reading the above description, some problems and questions demand attention. The main problem is that we are acquainted with the vocabulary and rules of modern science, yet, we don't know the vocabulary and rules of ancient science, all in Sanskrit, which was steeped in our tradition. Therefore, deep secrets would have to be decoded. Secondly, it was the custom to describe things in indirect, obscure and simileous manner so that the knowledge did not fall into the hands of the wrong person. Hence, to understand that too, the people who know both Sanskrit as well as technology need to make an effort.

METALS DESCRIBED IN THE *VIMANA SHASTRA*

The second question that arises is whether there is any

part of aeronautics, which could be proved initially through experimentation. If there is some part, then has any experiment been carried out in that direction? Was it successful?

Fortunately, the above questions can be answered in the affirmative. Dr. Sriram Prabhu of Hyderabad saw the chapter on the machine in *Vaimanic Shastra* and tried to recognise some of the 31 machines described in it and then experimented to find out if it was possible to make the alloys as described in its chapter on metals.

For experimental purposes, Dr. Prabhu and his colleagues began a project with the help from the B.M. Birla Science Centre, Hyderabad. Results obtained so far are promising.

They have been successful in making some metals on the basis of the descriptions in ancient scripture.

1. The first metal is *tamogarbh* iron. The *Viman Shastra* says that it is used to make aircrafts invisible. On exposing it to light, it absorbs 75-80 per cent of the light thrown on it. This metal is black in colour; hard like lead and it does not dissolve even in sulfuric acid.
2. The second is called the *panch lauh* or alloy of 5 items. It is golden in colour, but it is hard and heavy from inside. It is based on copper. Its specialty is that it has 7.95 per cent of lead, whereas the American Society of Metals in the US, has agreed that a maximum of 0.35 to 3 per cent of lead is possible in a copper based alloy. Hence, the alloy with 7.95 per cent lead is unique in itself.
3. The third is an *arar*. This is a copper-based alloy, which is yellow in colour, hard yet light. It has a property of resistance to moisture.

While informing the press on July 18, 1991 of

> the success in making these metals, Dr. B.B. Siddharth, Director, Birla Science Centre Hyderabad, said that in making these metals, various medicinal leaves, gum, barks of trees, etc. are also used. That is why while the production cost is less, some special qualities are developed in the metals. He further said that if the country's policy makers contemplate on the manufacture of the various metals described in the book and how to accumulate the necessary things, then it will be good for the future development of the country.[8]

The news of the above press conference was released by the news agency 'Varta'. It was published on July 19, in *Nai Duniya, MP Chronicle* and many other newspapers across the country.

In a similar fashion, Dr. Maheshwar Sheron of the Chemistry Department of IIT, Mumbai also tried to make some things described in the book. These were *chumbakmani,* which is used in the *guhagarbha yantra* and has the ability to capture reflection. *Paragrandhik drav* – this is a type of acid, which is used in the *guhagarbha,* and is used with a *chumbakmani.*[9]

Similarly, there is a description of the various kinds of metals and mirrors in Sage Bharadwaj's *Anshabodhini.* Dr. N.G. Dongre, Reader in the Harishchandra PG College, Varanasi, has undertaken a project with the cooperation of the Indian National Science Academy. The project was named 'The Study of Various Materials Discribed in *Anshabodhini* of Maharshi Bharadwaja'.

Under the project, he tried to make a mirror as described by Sage Bharadwaj, at the National Metallurgical Lab, Jamshedpur with the Director, P. Ramachandra Rao, who is at present the Vice-Chancellor of the Benaras Hindu

University. He was successful in manufacturing a special kind of glass called *prakash stambhan bhid lauh*. The specialty of this glass is that it absorbs visible light and allows only infra-red rays to pass through it.

It has been made of *kachar louh*-silica *bhuchakra surmitradikshar* – lime *ayaskakant* – lodestone *ruruk* – deerbone ash, as per the process laid down in *Anshabodhini*. The speciality of *prakash stambhan bhid lauh* is that it is completely non-hygroscopic. Infra-red hygroscopic mirrors lose their polish and lustre in water vapour or humidity and become useless. These days CaF_2 is extremely hygroscopic. Therefore, one has to be extra cautious while using these machines, although a study of the *prakash stambhan bhid lauh* has proved that it works best in the infra-red range of 2 to 5 microns (μ), where $1\ \mu = 10^{-4}$ cm, and that it can be used without worrying about the moisture in the atmosphere.[10]

Hence, we can say that the truth behind some of the experiments carried out in one of the chapters of Sage Bharadwaj's book make us believe that the others must also be true and that aeronautical science was not just an imagination in ancient times, but was a fact. The other chapters are also waiting for courageous researchers to prove them true.

□

8

Marine Science

The motto of the Indian Navy today is, "***Sham No Varunah***", which means – "Lord of the water be compassionate or kind to us". Journey by water has been a prevalent practice in India since the ancient times. Sage Agastya journeyed through the various islands in the oceans. That is why he is believed to have drunk all the water of an ocean. Indians travelled to various parts of the world to propagate their culture or for trade purposes. Kaundinya crossed the massive ocean and reached south-east Asia. In the rock inscriptions, in the Sun Temple, at Jawatuko in Yukatan province of Mexico, one finds mention of the arrival of the great sailor Vusulin in *Shaka Samvat* 854, that is, year 932. In the excavations in Lothal district in Gujarat, one believes that trade used to be carried on with Egypt from the port built around 2540 BC. From then till 2350 BC, small boats came to this port. Later, new constructions were erected necessary to harbour big ships and a city was built.

Similarly, the Malabar Coast in south India was also developed for trade purposes and to go to other countries *via* the sea. Thus, there has been a glorious history of boat and ship-building and voyages by sea.

Chamanlal, the famous Buddhist monk, mentioned the art of marine construction in his book *Hindu America*. Similarly, in 1950, Ganga Shankar Mishra written about this history in the *Hindu Sanskriti* edition of *Kalyana*.

Ships have also been talked about or mentioned in ancient Indian scriptures like the *Vedas, Brahmans, Ramayana, Mahabharata, Puranas*, etc. In the Ayodhya *kaand* of Valmiki's *Ramayana*, one reads of such big ships in which hundreds of warriors could ride –

"Navam Shatanam Panchanam Kaivartanam Shatam Shatam Sannatddhananam Tatha Yunantishthktivatyabhyachodayat."

"Hundreds of oarsmen inspire five hundred ships carrying hundreds of ready warriors."

Similarly, one finds the descriptions of a mechanical boat in the *Mahabharata* –

"Sarvavatasaham Navam Yantrayuktam Patakineen."

This is a boat with a mechanical flag (sail) which had the capacity to withstand all kinds of winds.

In the chapter on state administration in Kautilya's *Arthashaastra*, we get information in the context of the complete arrangements of boats maintained by the navy and the state.

Information on manufacturing of ships can be found in *Brihat Samhita*, written by Varahmihir in the 5th century and in the *Yukti Kalpataru*, written by Raja Bhoj in the 11th century.

The *Vriksha Ayurveda* talks about the kinds of wood. The soft wood which can be joined easily has been called the *brahmin*; the light, but stern wood which is difficult to join with other woods, has been called *kshatriya*; light and firm wood has been called *vaishya* and the heavy and firm wood has been called *shudra*. A wood having the qualities of two kinds of woods has been called *dwijaati*.

Bhoj, an expert on ships, says that a ship made of *kshatriya* wood is good. He also warns that iron should not be used in ships because it is likely that some of the sea rocks may have magnetic power. As such, they may pull the ships towards them. This may be dangerous for the ships.

TYPES OF SHIPS[1]

The *Yukti Kalpataru* has a detailed description of marine science and the kinds of ships, shapes and names have been analysed:

1. *Ordinary*—Those boats which can sail on ordinary rivers.
2. *Special*—On which voyages on the oceans can be carried out.

These boats and their shapes have been described as under:

Ordinary boats—the measurement is in **cubits.**

Name	**Length**	**Breadth**	**Height**
Kshudra	16	4	4
Madhyama	24	12	8
Bheema	40	20	20
Chapala	48	24	24
Patala	64	32	32
Bhaya	72	36	36
Deergha	88	44	44
Patraputa	96	48	48
Garbharaa	112	56	56
Manthara	120	60	60

The special boats have been divided into two categories:

1. *Deergha*
2. *Unnata*

There are ten kinds of *deerghas:*

1. *Deerghika*	32	4	$3\,{}^1/_5$
2. *Tarani*	48	6	$4\,{}^4/_5$
3. *Lola*	64	8	$6\,{}^2/_5$
4. *Gatvara*	80	10	8
5. *Gamini*	96	12	$9\,{}^2/_5$
6. *Tari*	112	14	$11\,{}^1/_5$
7. *Jangala*	128	16	$12\,{}^4/_5$
8. *Plavini*	144	18	$14\,{}^2/_5$
9. *Dharini*	160	20	16
10. *Vegini*	176	22	$17\,{}^3/_5$

Unnata is said to have five kinds:

1. *Oordhva*	22	16	16
2. *Anoordhva*	48	24	24
3. *Swarnamukhi*	64	32	32
4. *Garbhini*	80	40	40
5. *Manthara*	96	48	48

Excellent Construction[2]: The book gives a beautiful description of the decoration of the boat. A boat with four masts should be painted white; one with three masts should be red, one with two masts should be yellow and a boat with only one mast should be painted blue.

The prow of a boat[3]: There is a description of the front part of a boat in the shape of a lion, a buffalo, a snake, an elephant, a tiger, a bird, a frog, etc.

The boat has been in use in India since the Vedic age. The Muslim invasion started in India in the 7th century. Even at that time massive ships were built in India. Marco

Polo came to India in the 13th century. He writes, "Ships had double boards which were joined together. They were made strong with iron nails and the crevices were filled with a special kind of gum. These ships were so huge that about 300 boatmen were needed to row them. About 3000-4000 gunny bags could be loaded in each ship. They had many small rooms for people to live in. These rooms had arrangements for all kinds of comfort. When the bottom or the base started to get spoiled, a new layer would be added on. Sometimes, a boat would have even six layers, one on top of another."

A traveller named Nicolo Conti came to India in the 15th century. He wrote, "The Indian ships are much bigger than our ships. Their bases are made of three boards in such a way that they can face formidable storms. Some ships are made in such a way that if one part becomes useless, the rest of the parts can do the work."

Another traveller named Berthma writes, "The wooden boards are joined in such a way that not even a drop of water can go through it. Sometimes, the masts of cotton are placed in such a way that a lot of air can be filled in. The anchors were sometimes made of heavy stones. It would take a ship eight days to come from Iran to Cape Comorin (Kanyakumari)."

Kings of coastal regions had huge fleets of ships. In his book 'Indian Shipping', Dr. Radha Kumud Mukherji has given a very interesting and substantiated history of Indian ships.

DID VASCO DA GAMA DISCOVER THE ROUTE TO INDIA?[4]

Another illusion that the British spread was that Vasco da Gama discovered the sea route to India. It is true that Vasco da Gama came to India but if we get to know how he came, then reality will become clear.

The famous archeologist Padmashri Dr. Vishnu Shridhar Wakankar says, "I had gone to England for studies. I was told about Vasco da Gama's diary available in a museum in which he has described how he came to India." He writes that when his ship come near Zanzibar in Africa, he saw a ship three times bigger than the size of his ship. He took an African interpreter to meet the owner of that ship who was a Gujarati trader named Chandan who used to bring pine wood and teak from India along with spices and take back diamonds to the port of Cochin. When Vasco da Gama went to meet him, Chandan was sitting in ordinary attire, on a cot. When the trader asked Vasco where he was going, the latter said that he was going to visit India. At this, the trader said that he was going back to India the very next day and if he wanted, he could follow him. So, Vasco da Gama came to India following him. In independent India, this fact should have been told to the new generations but, unfortunately, this was not done.

As one reads this, the thought that can come to mind is that if India was so advanced in ship-building, then where did that knowledge disappear? From this point of view it is necessary to know the history of how the British came to India and planned to destroy the Indian shipping industry. Describing this history, Sh. Ganga Shankar Mishra writes[5]–

"Hindu Leading"– When the westerners made contact with India, they were amazed to see the ships here. Until the 17th century, European ships were a maximum of 600 tonnes. But in India, they saw such big ships as the *Gogha* which were more than 1500 tonnes. The European companies started using these ships and opened many new factories to make Indian artisans manufacture ships. In 1811, Lt. Walker writes, "The ships in the British fleet had to be repaired every 12th year. But the Indian ships made of teak would function for more than 50 years, without any repair." The East India Company had a ship called *Dariya Daulat* which worked for 87 years without any repairs. Durable woods like rosewood, sal and teak were used for this purpose.

The French traveller Waltzer Salvins writes, in his book *Le Hindu* in 1811 AD, "Hindus were in the forefront in the art of ship-building and even today, they can teach a lesson or two to the Europeans. The British, who were very apt at learning the arts, learnt a lot of things about ship building from the Hindus. There is a very good blend of beauty and utility in Indian ships and they are examples of Indian handicrafts and their patience." Between 1736 and 1863, 300 ships were built at factories in Mumbai. Many of them were included in the Royal Fleet. Of these, the ship called *Asia* was 2289 tonnes and had 84 cannons. Ship building factories were set up in Hoogly, Silhat, Chittagong, Dacca, etc. In the period between 1781 to 1821, in Hoogly alone 272 ships were manufactured which together weighed 1,22,693 tonnes.

THE CROOKEDNESS OF THE BRITISH

The shipping magnates of Britain could not tolerate the Indian art of ship manufacturing and they started compelling the East India Company not to use Indian ships. Investigations were frequently carried out in this regard. In 1811, Col. Walker gave statistics to prove that it was much cheaper to make Indian ships and that they were very sturdy. If only Indian ships were included in the British fleet, it would lead to great savings. This pinched the British ship-builders and the traders. Dr. Taylor writes "When the Indian ships laden with Indian goods reached the port of London, it created such a panic amongst the British traders as would not have been created, had they seen the enemy fleet of ships on the River Thames, ready for attack."

The workers at the London Port were among the first to make hue and cry and said that "all our work will be ruined and our families will starve to death." The Board of Directors of the East India Company wrote that "all the fear and respect that the Indian seamen had towards European behaviour was lost when they saw our social life once they came here. When they return to their country, they will propagate bad things about us amongst the Asians and we will lose our superiority and the effect will be harmful." At this, the British Parliament set up a committee under the chairmanship of Sir Robert Peel.

Black Law: Despite disagreement amongst the members of the committee on the basis of this report, a law was passed in 1814 according to which the Indians lost the right to become British sailors and it became compulsory to employ at least three-fourth British sailors on British ships. No ship, which did not have a British master, was allowed to enter London Port and a rule was made that only ships made by the British in England could bring goods to England. For many reasons, there was laxity in enforcing these rules but from 1863, they were observed strictly. Such rules which would end the ancient art of ship-building, were formulated in India also. Tax on goods brought in Indian ships was raised and efforts were made to isolate them from trade. Sir William Digby has rightly written, "This way, the Queen of the western world killed the Queen of the eastern oceans."

In short, this is the story about the destruction of the Indian art of ship-building.

□

9

Garment Industry

In an article written in *Bhumiputra* on June 16, 1986, Vinoba Bhave has described how clothes started being made. The basis of the garment industry is thread which is made from cotton. The *Vedas* say that Sage Gritsmad was the first to sow cotton and obtained 10 *sers* (1 ser = 0.8 kg) of cotton wool. With this, he made thread. Then he had a problem of how to make cloth. He made a wooden bobbin and with the ***tantu*** (raw thread), he made cloth. Thus, the process of making cloth from thread was started by Sage Gritsmad.

Later, with progress and development, cloth started to be made from silk, *kosa* etc. and clothes and sarees thus made, began to be coloured and embroidered with gold, silver, etc. Clothes were dyed with natural colours. At one time, Indian cloth was exported to virtually all the countries of the world. Traders from ancient Greece, Egypt and Arabia started ordering cotton cloth from India, especially the *mulmul* from Bengal, which became famous throughout the world as Dacca *mulmul*. These traders used to sell this cloth in the various provinces and cities of their countries.

With respect to the speciality of Indian clothes, Pramod Kumar Dutt gives observations of various people and writes –

"Two Arab travellers came here in the 9th century. They wrote that the Indian clothes were so extraordinary, that one could not find such clothes anywhere. The cloth is so fine and beautiful that an entire length can be passed through a ring."

Marco Polo, who came in the 13th century, made a unique announcement that "Coromandal and Macchalipattanam coasts were the places of production for all types of beautiful, fine clothes found in any corner of the world."

Various interesting stories about fineness and clarity of the cloth are famous. Once, Aurangzeb's daughter went to court (*Darbar*). Aurangzeb was very angry to see her clothes and said, "Have you lost all sense of shame that you are showing your body to the whole world?" At this, his daughter said, "What can I do, father! I have folded the cloth seven times over and then worn it."

The French traveller and trader, Tavernier, who came to visit central India in the 17th century, while describing cotton clothes, writes, "They are so light and beautiful that you cannot even feel them with your hands and the delicate embroidery is hardly visible." He adds, "The cotton manufactured in Sikanj (in Malwa Province), like the one in Calicut, is so fine that the wearer's body is visible as if he is naked." He writes in another edition, "A Persian Ambassador went back from India and gifted a coconut to his Sultan. The courtiers were amazed at this petty gift. But more amazing was the fact that when the coconut was opened, a roll of 30 yards of *mulmul* came out of it." M. Wilkins gave a piece of Dacca mulmul to Sir Joseph Bake who said that it was an excellent sample of the fineness of cloth in the recent past. He measured the sample himself and sent his analysis to India House. It was as follows–

Mr. Bake says that the piece of cloth given by Wilkins weighed 34.3 grains (7000 grains=1 pound and 15.5 grains =1 gm.). Its length was 5 yards 7 inches and it had 198 threads. This meant that the total length of the thread was 1028.5 yards, and that 29.98 yards of thread were made from 1 grain and that the thread was of 2425 counts. In modern technology too, a thread is not finer than 500-600 counts.[1]

On the request of the Secretary of State of India, Sir G. Birdwood had written a book entitled *The Industrial Arts of India*. On page 83 of this book, he writes that "it is said that during Jehangir's reign, 15 yards long and 1 yard wide Dacca *mulmul* weighed only 100 grains."

On page 95 of the same book, it is written, "The British and the European authors have made poetic similes of the *mulmul*, the cotton and the silk cloth to a 'bulbul's eye', 'the throat of a peacock', 'the moon and the stars', *Bafte Hava* (The stars of the wind), 'Flowing water' and 'Evening dew'. Production of cotton cloth and *mulmul* started in England in 1772 and 1781 respectively.

In 1835, Edward Benz wrote, "The Indians in every age have, in the textile industry, maintained an incomparable and matchless standard. Some of their *mulmul* clothes seem to have been made, not by humans but by fairies and butterflies."

By conspiracy, the British destroyed the cottage industry where such fine clothes were manufactured; they cut off the thumbs that made them.

It was hoped that after the country became independent, we would go back to our roots and get back the thumbs that were cut off, but, even today, our country remains under the halo of western technology. We need to consider changing this. □

10

Mathematics

We, in India, have had a tradition of science from ancient times. A *shloka* which interprets or establishes the importance of mathematics, is prevalent since ancient times.

> ***Yatha shikha mayuranam naganam manayo yatha***
> ***Tadvad vedangshastranam ganitam moordhani sthitam.***
>
> – *(Yajush jyotisham)*

The *shloka* says that just as the crest of the peacock and the gem of the cobra, stays right at the top, similarly mathematics is established right at the topmost position in the *Vedas* and the *shastras*.

In the *mantra* for peace, in the *Eishavasyopanishad,* it is said –

> ***Aum poornamadah poornamidam poornat poornamudchyate***
> ***Poornasya poornamadaya poornamevavashishyate***

This *mantra* is not just a spiritual description. Instead, it has an extremely important mathematical sign hidden in it. This became the base or the foundation of all mathematics. The *mantra* says: this is complete, that is complete. A whole is born out of a whole, yet it is a whole and, even in the end, when the whole is merged within the whole, it still remains a whole. The characeteristic of a whole is present in zero and in the infinite too. If you add or subtract a zero to or from a zero, what remains is a zero only. The same is the case with the infinite.

In the case of the world, we have had two kinds of thinkers- *iti-* the one who said something about completeness and the other was *neti-* the one who said something about the zero. The invention of the zero has been unique from the point of view of counting and in the development of mathematics.

India has been the father of mathematics. Even the world acknowledges it. The oldest European book on mathematics is *Coda Vigilanus,* which is kept in the Museum in the Spanish capital of Madrid. In this, it is written—

"From the signs of counting (numerals), we experience that the ancient Hindus had very sharp brains and that the other countries were much behind them in counting and in geometry and other sciences. This is proved by their nine numerals with the help of which any number can be written."

Modern scientists Laplace and Albert Einstien have wholeheartedly praised the significant role that the combination of the nine digits and the zero has played in making innumerable calculations and in the scientific development of the world.

Many scholars have described the journey of the Indian numerals throughout the world. A brief mention of it has been made by Bharti Krishna Teerthaji, the Shankaracharya of Puri in the foreward of his amazing book on mathematics called *Vedic Mathematics*.

He writes, "It gives me great pleasure to say that some well known modern mathematicians like Prof. G.P. Halstand, Prof. D. Morgan and Prof. Hutton, who are researchers and lovers of truth have, in contrast to Indian scholars, adopted a scientific outlook and have wholeheartedly praised India's unique contribution to the progress of mathematical knowledge."[1]

The examples of some of the scholars will present ample explicit proofs themselves.

1. On page 20 of his book *The Foundation and Process of Mathematics*, Prof. G.P. Halstand says, "The significance or importance of the discovery of the zero can never be explained. Giving not just a name but authority, in fact, power to 'nothing', is the characteristic of the Hindu community, whose invention, it is. It is like giving the power of the dynamo to *nirvana* or salvation. No other single mathematical invention has been more effective than this in the general development or progress of intelligence and power."
2. In the same context, B.B. Dutt, in his narrative, "The modern way to express numerals" (*Indian Historical Quarterly*, Issue-3, pp. 530-540) says, "The Hindus had adopted the 'Decimal System' a long time back. The numerical language of no other country had been able to achieve or acquire the scientific calibre and the completeness that ancient India had. The ancient Indians had achieved success in expressing any number beautifully and easily with the help of only ten symbols. The beauty of Hindu numeral markings attracted the civilised world and they gladly adopted it."

3. In his article 'New Light on our Numerals' published in *The bulletin of the American Mathematical Society* pp. 366-369, Prof. Ginsberg says, "In around 770 AD, Abba Sayeed Khalifa Al-Mansur of Baghdad had invited the famous Hindu scholar Kank of Ujjain to the famous court of Baghdad. This is how the Hindu way of marking numerals reached Baghdad. Kank taught Hindu astrology and mathematics to the Arab scholars. With Kank's help they even translated Brahmagupta's *Brahma Sphut Siddhant* into Arabic. French scholar M.F. Nau's latest discovery proves that Indian numerals were known in Syria in the 7th century and were also praised."
4. In his essay, B.B. Dutt further writes, "These numerals slowly reached the west *via* north Arabia and Egypt and by the 11th century reached Europe. The Europeans called them Arabic numerals because they got them from Arabia but the Arabs themselves unanimously called them Hindu numerals." (Al-Arkan – Al-Hind)

The Decimal System: *Ekam* of Sanskrit became *ek* in Hindi and 'one' in Arabic and Greek while the *shunya* became *sifar* in Arabis, *jeefar* in Greek and 'zero' in English. This is how Indian numerals spread throughout the world.

Arithmetic: The sequence-wise description of the numbers can be found in the *Yajurveda:*

Savita prathameahannagni rdviteeye vayustriteeya
Aadityenchaturthe chandramaah
Panchamarituh shashthe marootah saptame brahaspatirashtame
Mitro navame varuno dashamam indra ekaadashe
Vishwedeva dwadashe

– *(Yajurveda 39-6)*

What is special is that the numbers are given here from one to twelve in a sequence.

From the aspect of counting, the largest number known to the ancient Greeks was myriad which is equal to 10^4 or 10,000 and the largest number known to the Romans was 10^3, i.e. 1000. On the contrary, many kinds of counting were prevalent in India. These methods were independent. The methods described in the Vedic, Buddhist and Jain texts, have a similarity in the names of some of the numbers but there is a difference in the value of the numbers.

First: Next number multiple of 10: This means that the number that comes next is 10 times more. The second mantra in the 17th chapter of the *Yajurveda Samhita* refers to this, whose sequence is given–*Ek, dash, shat, sahastra, ayut, niyut, prayut, arbud, nyarbud, samudra, madhya, ananta* and *parardh*. In this way, *Parardh* measured 10^{12} that is one thousand billion or one trillion (US).

Second: Next number multiple of 100: This means that the next number is 100 times more than the earlier number. In this context, we must refer to the coversation between mathematician Arjun and Bodhisatva in *Lalit Vistar,* the Buddhist text from the 1st century BC in which he asks what the number after 1 crore is? In reply, Bodhisatva describes the numbers after crore, which are multiples of 100.

Shat (One hundred) *koti = ayut, niyut, kankar, vivar, kshomya, nivaah, utsang, bahul, naagbal, titilamb, vyavasthanapragyapti, hetusheel, karahu, hetvindriya, samaaptalambh, gananagati, nikhadh, mudraabal, sarvabal, vishagyagati, sarvagya, vibhutangama and tallakshana* which meant that *tallakshana* means 10 raised to the power of 53. (i.e. 10^{53})

Third: Next number multiple of ten million: The 51st and 52nd chapters of Katyayan's Pali Grammar has reference to multiples of crores, i.e. the next number is a crore times (i.e. 10^7 times) more than the earlier number.

In this centext, the Jain text of *Anuyugodwar* describes the numbers after *koti* as follows—

> ***Koti koti, pakoti, kotyapakoti, nahut, ninnahut, akkhobhini, bindu, abbnd, nirashbud, ahah, abab, atat, sogandhik, uppalkumud, pundareek, padum, kathaan, mahakathaan and asankhyeya.***

Asankhyeya measures 10^{140} that means 10 raised to power of 140.

From the above description, it becomes quite clear as to how much developed was the knowledge of numbers in India in the ancient times while the rest of the world did not know more than 10,000.

The above references have been given in detail in Vibhootibhushan Dutt and Avadhesh Narayan Singh's book *The History of Hindu Mathematics*.

Later on, many mathematicians like Aryabhatta, Bhaskaracharya, Shridhar, etc. were seen in the country. Of them Bhaskaracharya wrote *Siddhanth Shiromani* in 1150. This great book has four parts: (1) Leelavati, (2) Algebra, (3) Goladhyaya, and (4) Graha Ganit.

In his book *Bhaskaracharya,* Shri Gunakar Muley writes that Bhaskaracharya has acknowledged the basic eight works of mathematics:

1. Addition
2. Subtraction
3. Multiplication
4. Division
5. Square
6. Square Root
7. Cube
8. Cube root.

All these mathematical calculations were prevalent in India for thousands of years. However, Bhaskaracharya tells Leelavati a strange thing, "At the root of all these calculations there are only two basic calculations – rise and fall or increase and decrease. Addition is increasing and subtraction is decreasing. The entire mathematics permeates from these two basic acts."

These days, the computer solves the biggest and the most difficult calculations in a short time. All calculations are made with only two signs of addition and subtraction (+ and -). These are turned into electric signals i.e., the positive flow for addition and the reverse flow for subtraction. With this, calculations can be made at the speed of lightning. We understand increase, decrease, one and zero today but Bhaskaracharya had the basic knowledge at that time.

These days, mathematics is considered a dry subject. But Bhaskaracharya's *Leelavati* is an example of how it can be taught with fun by intermixing it with entertainment, curiosity, etc. Let us see an example from Leelavati:

"From a bunch of pure lotuses' $^1/_3$, $^1/_5$, and $^1/_6$ parts were used for the worship of Shiv, Vishnu and Durga respectively; ¼ was used to worship Parvati and the 6 that were left, were used for the worship of the guru's feet. Now, Leelavati, quickly tell me how many lotus flowers were there in the bunch?" The answer is 120 flowers.

Explaining the square and the cube, Bhaskaracharya says, "Leelavati, a square shape and its area are called the square. The multiplication of two equal numbers is also called a square. Similarly, the multiplication of three equal numbers is called cube and a solid with 12 compartments and equal arms is also called a cube."

'*Mool*' or root in Sanskrit, meant the root of a tree or plant or, in a more expansive form, it means cause of something or origin also. Hence, in ancient mathematics, square root meant the reason for the square or origin that is one arm of a square. Likewise, we can understand the meaning of cube root in the same way. A number of ways were prevalent to find out the cube root and the square root.

In the same way, Bhaskaracharya mentions the trairashik. It had trinomial sums hence its name. For example, if one gets *'pr'* (as in *pramaan)* in *'ph'* (as in *phal*), then what will we find in *'i'* (as in *ichchha,* that is desire)?

In *trairaashik* [trinomial] questions, the *phal* number should be multiplied by the *ichchha* number and the result should be divided by the *pramaan* number. What is thus acquired is the *itccha phal* (desired fruit). About 2000 years ago, the *trairaashik [trinomial] rule* was discovered in India. It reached the Arab countries in the 8th century AD. The Arab mathematicians called the *trairaashik* ***'fee raashikaat al hind'***. Later, it spread to Europe where it was given the title of the Golden Rule.

The ancient mathematicians had knowledge not only of the *trairaashik* but also of the *pancharaashik, saptaraashik* and the *navaraashik.* (penta-or quinqnomial, hepta or septunomial and nonomial)

ALGEBRA

India is the birthplace of algebra. It was called indistinct or cryptic mathematics. The Arab scholar Moosa-Al-Khawarizmi came to India in the 9th century to learn this and wrote a book called *Alijeb Oyal Muquabila*. Thence, this knowledge went to Europe.

In ancient times, mathematicians such as Aapastamba, Bodhaayan, Katyaayan and later, Brahmagupta and Bhaskaracharya worked on algebra.

Bhaskaracharya says that algebra means unexpressed

mathematics but the initial reason is expressed. Hence, in Leelavati, arithmetic, which was expressed mathematics, was discussed at the start.

In algebra, Bhaskaracharya talks about zero and infinity.

Vadha au viyat khan khenadhaate, khaharo bhavet khen bhaktashch raashih

This means that if zero is divided by any number or multiplied by any number, the result is zero. If any number is divided by zero, the result is infinity.

Zero and infinity are the two precious jewels of mathematics. Life can continue without jewels but mathematics is nothing without zero and infinity.

Zero and infinity have no place or name in the physical world and are only the creations of the human mind. Yet, through the medium of mathematics and science, they clarify even the most difficult mysteries of the world.

Brahmagupta discovered various equations. He gave them the names of *ek varna, anek varna, madhyamaharan* and *mapit*. There is one unknown number in an *ek varna* equation and many unknown numbers in *anek varna*.

GEOMETRY

India is the birthplace of geometry also. Since antiquity, altars and platforms were made for religious ceremonies. Their basis was geometry. In 800 BC, Bodhayan and Aapastamb gave the necessary architectural specifications for the construction of these altars and platforms.

Drawing a square equal to a triangle, a square which is double, triple or one-third a square. Making a circle equal in area to the square present. These methods have been explained in the *Shulbhasootra*.

The method of how to find the area of a triangle from its sides, has been explained in the 4th century book *Soorya Siddhanta*. Europe got this knowledge from Clobius in the 16th century.

VOYAGE OF A WORD[2]

In our country, the bow is called *jya*. We used this word in geometry. When it reached Arabia, it became 'j' and 'b', since they don't have vowels like 'e' and 'u'. When it reached Europe, it began to be called 'jeb', which means 'chest'. The word for chest in Latin is 'sinus'. So, in short, it started being called 'sine'. Many such words have travelled from India to Europe *via* Arabia.

PYTHAGORAS' THEOREM OR BODHAYAN THEOREM

In many chapters of the Kalpasootra scriptures there is a chapter on *shulbasootra*. The rope used to measure the platform is called *rajjoo* or *shulbha*. Hence, geometry is also called shulba and the subject of geometry came under *shulbasootra*. The Bodhayan Theorem is as under:

> ***Deerghachaturas Syaakshanaya Rajjooha Pashrvamaani Tiryakmaani***
> ***Yatprithagbhoote Kurutasta Dubhayam Karoti***
>
> – (*Bodhayan Shulbhasootra* 1-12)

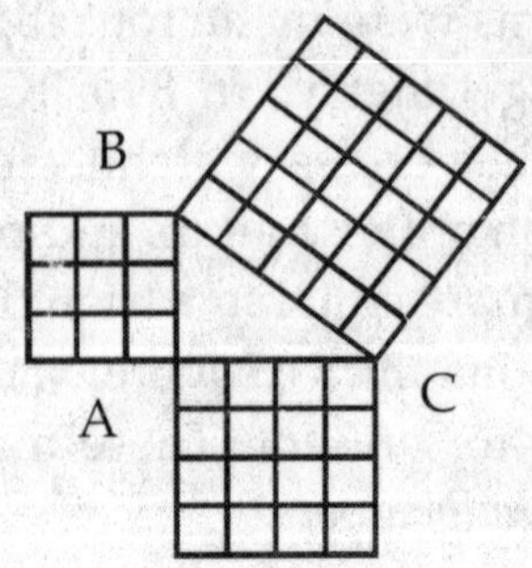

This means that the area of hypotenuse in a triangle is equal to the area of its length and breadth. Bodhayan has given this principle in the *Shulbasootra.* When we read this, we understand that if the hypotenuse of a triangle is BC, length is AB and breadth is AC, then the Bodhayan Theorem says,

$BC^2 = AB^2 + AC^2$.

This is taught to the students today as Pythagoras' Theorem, whereas it had been described by Bodhayan at least 1000 years before the Greek mathematician Pythagoras. It is also possible that Pythagoras worked out this theorem after reading about it in the *Shulbasootra.* Whatever it is, there is no argument about the fact that the Indian mathematicians were far ahead of the modern mathematicians in the field of geometry. Besides the above mentioned theorem, Bodhayan has given other theorems too. The diagonal of a rectangle, divides it into two equal parts and two diagonals of a rectangle divide each other equally. The diagonals of a square cross each other at right angles, etc. Bodhayan and Apastamba both have given the ratio of the arm and the diagonal of a rectangle which is exactly correct.

Shulbasootra tells one how to make a square of the same area as that of a triangle, a circle of the same area as that of a square, and make a circle double, triple or one third of the area of a square. Bhaskaracharya's *Leelavati* tells us that an arm of an equal tetragon, pentagon, hexagon, octagon in a circle, is in definite proportions to the diameter of the circle.

Aryabhatt has also given a formula for calculating the area of a triangle. It is as follows:

Tribhajasya phalashareeram samadal koti bhajardhasamvargaha

The area of a triangle is equal to the product of the length and half of the base of the triangle. As per the diagram given here, the area of the triangle ABC = ½ AB × CP.

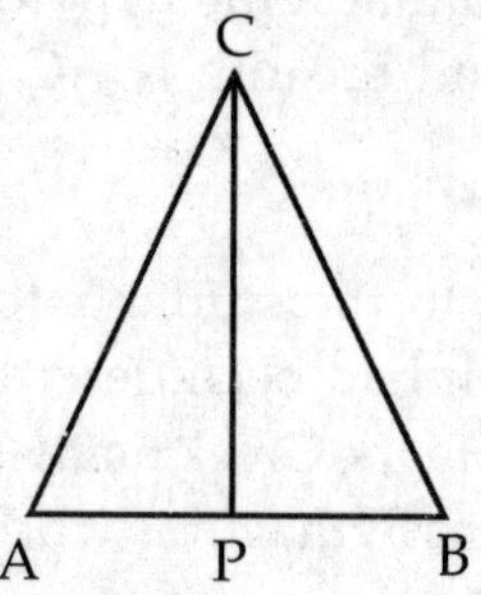

THE VALUE OF pi (π)

About 1500 years ago, Aryabhatta had calculated the value of pi acurately.

Today, the ratio between the diameter and the circumference of a circle is called pi. Earlier, the measurement was estimated as the square root of 10. The first number of the product of one number, multiplied by itself becomes the square root. Eg. 2 × 2 = 4. Hence, 2 is the square root of 4. However, although it is difficult to give the right value of the square root of 10, yet, for calculation, it is important to know the nearest value. Aryabhatta puts this as:

> ***Chaturadhikam Shatmashtagunam Dwashashtisthta Sahsranam***
> ***Ayutdvayanishkambhsyasanno Vrittaparinahaha.***
>
> — *(Aryabhattiya – 10)*

If the diameter of a circle is 20,000, then its circumference will be 62832.

$$\therefore \pi = \frac{\text{Circumference}}{\text{Diameter}} = \frac{62832}{20000} = 3.1416$$

Aryabhatta does not consider this value as pure and exact, but approximate. This shows how insisitent he was about truth.

Abul Fazal, a minister in Akbar's court wrote about the incidents of his time in his *Ain-i-Akbari*. He writes that the Greeks did not know that the Hindus had found out the mysterious relationship between the diameter and the circumference of a circle. Aryabhatta is supposed to be the first man to talk about the value of pi.

TRIGONOMETRY

Bodhayan's theorem is the basis of trignometry. Hence, the principles of trigonometry have naturally been given in the *Shulbasootra*. India's *jya* and *Kotijya* became sine and cosine on going to the West. Actually the word *jya* has come from a bowstring. In the picture that appears below, CA is like a half circle or bow and AP is like its string (*jya*). BP has been called *kotjya*. The Indian scholars had the knowledge to work out the value of *kotjya* (BP) and *jya* (AP) from the radius of the circle. If we assume angle ABP to be Q then Aryabhatta had calculated the value of *jya* and *kotjya* according to the angle Q. Aryabhatta said that the value of AP was *trijya* (BA) × *jya* (Q) and the value of RA (BP) was *trijya* (BA) × *kotjya* (Q). According to today's trignometry, it is written as:

Height (AP) = hypotenuse × sin Q

$$\left(\text{or } \sin Q = \frac{\text{height}}{\text{hypotenuse}}\right)$$

Base BP = hypotenuse × cosine Q

$$\left(\text{or } \cos Q = \frac{\text{base}}{\text{hypotenuse}}\right)$$

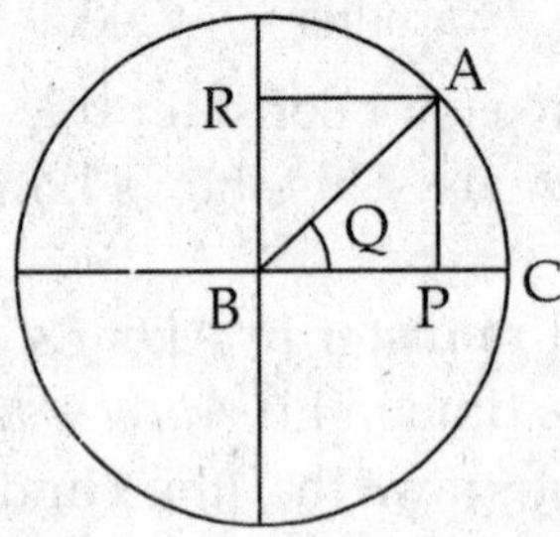

Aryabhatta found out the value of sine for the various angles, from 0° to 90° and made a table for it too. There is a very interesting question in Bhaskaracharya's *Leelavati*. Two monkeys are sitting on a tree which is 2000 inches high (DB). About 4000 inches away, there is a well (C). One monkey climbs down from the tree and goes to the well. The other monkey climbs to a set height (A) and jumps straight into the well. If the distance covered by the two monkeys is the same (DB + BC = DA + AC), then how high did the other monkey jump? Or how much is AD? This question definitely belongs to trigonometry and the distance covered comes out to be 5000 inches. It is quite clear that Bhaskaracharya has described all the principles of trigonometry in *Leelavati*.

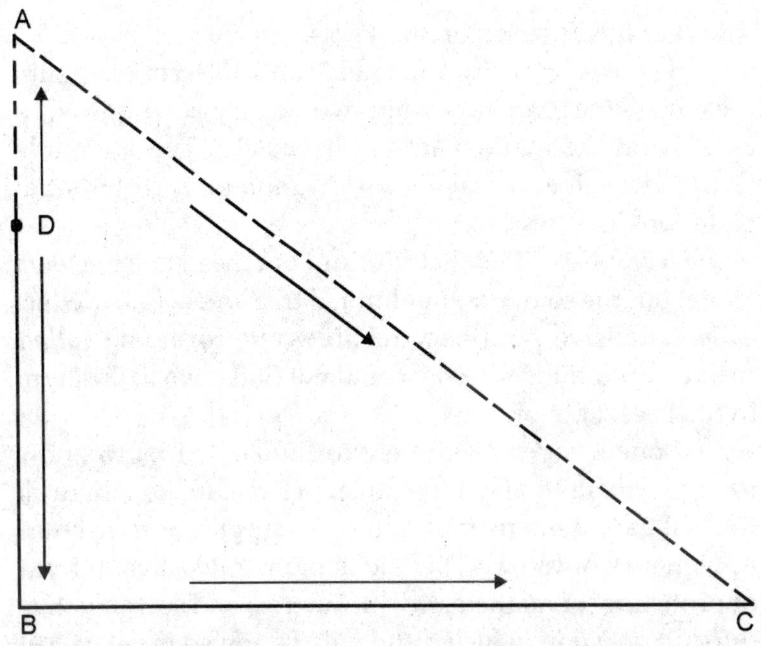

In the 4th part of his book *Siddhant Shiromani*, on astrological calculations, Bhaskaracharya has used differentiation to find out the speed of a planet. This part of mathematics, i.e. calculus, is the basis of modern science and technology. Liebatanis and Newton are considered fathers of calculus. Five hundred years before these two, Bhaskaracharya had used calculus to find the speed of the planets. Thus we know about Indian superiority in the field of mathematics.

VEDIC MATHEMATICS

After eight years of devoted practice, Shankaracharya Bharti Krishna Teerthaji of Puri discovered a new mathematical process which he called "Mathetmatics Without Tears!", which was not dry, sad or troublesome, but easy and enjoyable. He called it Vedic Mathematics and said that it was based on the *Vedas*.

He gave 16 primary formulae and 13 secondary sub-formulae – the practice of which would help solve questions of 10 kinds of mathematics, very easily. These include arithmetic, algebra, geometry, trignometry, differential equations, calculus, etc.

Here, he clarified that *Veda* did not mean mere *samhita* (code) but the source and unlimited treasure of knowledge. This expansive periphery includes the formulae called mathematics, although one would not find them in this form in the present books.

If one has practised these formulae and knows how to apply them, one can get amazing results. Jagadguruji himself gave demonstrations on their applications in some universities of India. When he demonstrated this in front of professors of mathematics in America and solved a very difficult question (which could only be solved in 3-4 pages) on the blackboard, the audience was utterly surprised.

Professor Nicholas of England calls it magic and not mere mathematics. When people asked Jagadguru Bharti Krishna Teerthji if it was mathematics or magic, he would say that until you do not know it, it is magic; when you get to know it, it is mathematics.

If this method is taught from the very beginning, interest in mathematics may increase. Many scholars are researching this subject and are developing ways of learning it. (Although Vedic Mathematics is not yet included in formal syllabus, a very interesting trend is becoming popular – coaching institutes for various competitive exams are teaching Vedic Mathematics and the results are very encouraging.)

Those amazing 16 mathematical formulae and the 13 sub-formulae, along with their meanings are given below:

16 FORMULAE OF VEDIC MATHEMATICS AND THEIR MEANINGS

1. *Ekadhiken Poorven*	By one more than the previous one.
2. *Nikhilam Navtashcharam Dashtaha*	All from nine and last from ten.
3. *Oordhvatiryak Bhyam*	Vertically and cross-wise.
4. *Paravartya Yojayet*	Transpose and apply.
5. *Shoonyam Saamyasamuchhaye*	When the *samuchchaya* is the same then that is zero.
6. *Aanurroopye Shoonyamanyata*	If one is in ratio, the other one is zero.
7. *Sankalanvyavakalanabhyam*	By addition and subtraction.
8. *Poornapoornabhyam*	By completion and non-completion.
9. *Chalankalanabhyam*	By sequential motion.
10. *Yavadoonam*	The deficiency.
11. *Vyashtisamashti*	Whole as one and one as whole.
12. *Seshanyanken Charamen*	Remainder by the last.
13. *Sopantyadvayamantyam*	Ultimate and twice the penultimate.
14. *Ekanyoonen Poorven*	By one less than the previous one.
15. *Ganitasamuchyah*	The whole product.
16. *Gunakasyamuchyah*	Collectivity of multipliers.

SUB-FORMULAE

1. *Anuroopyen*	Through conformity
2. *Shishyate Sheshsangaha*	The remaining one is called *shesh*.
3. *Aadyamaadyenantayamantyen*	First with the first, last with the last one.
4. *Kevalaiyah Saptakam Gunyat*	Multiply *ka* (1) *va* (4), *la* (3) by 7 (formula for 1/7).
5. *Veshtanam*	The osculation (A method for divisibility test).
6. *Yavadoonam Tavadoonam*	Whatever deficiency, further lessen that much.
7. *Yavadoonam Tavadoonikritya Varga cha yojayet*	Lessen by the deficiency and use its square.
8. *Antyordashakeapi*	Sum of the last digits is ten.
9. *Antyayorev*	Only by the last.
10. *Samucchayegunitaha*	Product of whole.
11. *Lopanasthapanabhyam*	By alternating elimination and retention.
12. *Vilokanam*	By glancing.
13. *Gunitasmuchhayaha Samuchhayagunitaha*	Product of the whole is equal to whole of the product.

□

11

Measurement of Time

When was the world created and till when will it last? These questions have been disturbing man for ages. To get the answers, we will first have to understand time. Time – through which we measure incidents and changes; when did it start?

Stephen Hawkings, the renowned cosmologist of modern times, has written a book on this. It is called *The Brief History of Time*. In this book, he writes that universe and time started together when the Big Bang occurred. This resulted in the creation of the universe and the universe came from the unexpressed state into the expressed state. With this, time was also born. Hence, the universe and time started together and shall remain so until the universe survives and shall vanish with it. The second question is 'What was there before the universe? In reply, Hawkings says that today that is unknown. However, there can be a way to find out. A star dies when its fuel is used up in the form of light and energy and it starts shrinking until it beomes a dot. At that time, it acquires such a strong gravitational force that it can absorb light. It thus becomes impossible to know what is inside. Lack of light is known as darkness. It is probably because of this that such areas are called black holes. Our universe too perhaps was in this condition before being born.

In India, sages contemplated on this and perceived it. Describing the condition before the creation of the universe, the *Naasadiya Sookta* of the *Rigveda* says that there was no truth or untruth, neither atom nor leisure. Then what was there? There was neither death nor immortality, neither day nor night. At that time, there was an element with the power of pulsation.

Darkness was enveloped with the darkness before creation and there was an element which had the power or the strength of penance. It was first the power of the effect of desire that the equilibrium was shattered and the universe was created from the unexpressed state. And the journey of time also began. This is how the journey of the time moves on along with the universe.

Defining this, Sages have described it as 'kalayati sarvaani bhootani' that is one that drives the entire universe or creation. It is also said that this universe is made once and then, gets destroyed, this is not the end. The cycle of birth and death, creation and destruction goes on. The giant wheel of time goes on with its creation, position, change and destruction. The poets of India and the west have described the all-eclipsing form of time alike. Kshemendra, a renowned poet of India has expressed his views thus-

Aho kaalasamudrasya na lakshyante atisantataah
Majjantontaranantasya yugaantaah parvataa iva.

"There is no such interval as compression in the ocean of time; huge mountains like massive ages come to submerge into it." Octavia Paz, the poet who won the Nobel Prize in 1990, has, in his poem 'Into the Matter', described the all engulfing nature of time in the following words –

A clock strikes the time
Now it's time
It is not time now, not it is now
Now it is time to get rid of time
Now it is not time
It is time and not now
Time eats the now

Now it is time
Windows close
Walls closed doors close
The words go home
Now we are more alone[1].......

The shortest as well as the largest unit of time has been described in our country.

There is a reference to this in the *Shrimad Bhagwad Mahapurana*. King Pareekshit asks Sage Shukdev what is time? What are its minutest and greatest forms? The reply that the sage gives is amazing because in today's modern age, we know that time is an abstract element. We know it because of the incidents that occur. Thousands of years ago, Sage Shukdev had said, "The changing of subjects is the form of time. The element of time expresses itself through it (change). It expresses itself through the unexpressed."

MEASUREMENT OF TIME

The minutest part of time is the atom and the greatest is *Brahma* Age. Explaining it in detail, Sage Shuk gives its various measures –

2 *paramaanu* – 1 *Anu*	15 *laghu* – 1 *naarikaa*
3 *Anu* –1 *trasrenu*	2 *naadikaa* – 1*muhoort*
3 *trasrenu* –1 *truti*	30 *muhoort* – 1 day-night
100 *truti* – 1 *vedh*	7 day-night – 1 week
3 *vedh* – 1 *lav*	2 weeks – 1 fortnight
3 *lav* – 1 *nimesh*	2 fortnights – 1 month
3 *nimesh* – 1 *kshan* (moment)	2 months – 1 *ritu* (season)
5 *kshan* – 1 *kaashthaa*	3 *ritus* – 1 *ayan*
15 *kaashthaa* – 1 *laghu*	2 *ayans* – 1 year

According to the calculations of Sage Shuk, there are 3280500000 *paramaanu* of time in a day and night and 86,400 seconds in a day and night. This means that in its minutest measure, one *paramaanu* of time is equal to 37968th part of a second.

In A 231 of the *Moksh Parva* in the *Mahabharata*, time has been calculated as under—

15 *nimesh* –1 *kaashtha*
30 *kaashthaa* – 1 *kala*
30 *kala* – 1 *muhoort*
30 *muhoort* –1 day and night

There is a slight difference between the two calculations. According to Sage Shuk, there are 450 *kaashthaas* in a moment and according to the *Mahabharata*, there are 900 *kaashhaas* in a moment. This implies the different methods of calculations.

These are the units for ordinary time calculations. But to measure the age of the universe or the changes therein, bigger units will be required. That measurement unit is *yug*.

Kaliyug	432,000 years
2 *Kaliyug*	*Dwaparyug* 864,000 years
3 *Kaliyug*	*Tretayug* 1296,000 years

4 *Kaliyug* *Satyug* 1728,000 years

The four ages together make a *Chaturyugi* 4320,000

71 *Chaturyugis* make a *Manvantar* 306720,000

14 *Manvantaras* along with 15 *Satyugs* as a part of the dusk make up a *kalp* that is 4320,000,000 years.

One *kalpa* means one day of Brahma. One night of His is equally long. One Brahma lives for 100 years and when one Brahma dies, it is Lord Vishnu's *nimesh* (blinking of the eye), and after Vishnu, the age of Rudra starts. He is himself a form of *kaal* and is, therefore, eternal. That is why time is said to be endless.

After reading this description of Sage Shukdev, a thought that comes to mind is that this discription is fantastic imagination and an intellectual game. What is the significance of such things in today's scientific age? But this is not fantastic imagination. It is related to astronomy. India's calculations of time were made on the basis of a minute study of the speed and changes in the astronomical bodies which means solid scientific truth; whereas in the calculations of the **Anno Domini era** prevalent today, the only scientific thing is the fact that the year is based on the calculations of the time that the earth takes to revolve around the sun. Otherwise, there is no relation between the calculations of the months and days and astronomical speeds.

Let us try to find out something about the Western and Indian calculations of time.

HISTORY OF MEASUREMENT OF TIME IN THE WEST

In the context of the calendar, Vol. 3-1964 of the children's *Britannica* gives a brief description of its history. Calendar means a way of dividing time on the basis of year, month, days, the movement of the earth and the moon. *Luna* is the Latin word for the moon. Hence, it is known as the Lunar month. The Latin word for sun is *Sol*; therefore we call it a solar year.

Today, it measures 365 days, 5 hours, 48 minutes and 46 seconds. Since there is no co-ordination between the solar year and the lunar month, there was confusion or disorder in many countries. Another reason for this confusion was the lack of knowledge.

Secondly, comes the point of dividing time on the basis of a historical event, Christians believe that the birth of Christ is the deciding event of history. On this basis, they divided history into two parts - (1) BC, which means the period before the birth of Christ and refers to incidents that took place before the birth of Christ, and (2) The events that occurred after the birth of Christ are called AD which stands for **Anno Domini** which means **in the year of our Lord.** It is a different matter that this method was not in use for some centuries after the birth of Christ.

ROMAN CALENDAR

Todays's AD year is based on the Roman calendar. It started with the establishment of the city of Rome - 753 years before the birth of Christ. Initially it had a 10 month year which lasted from March till December and had 304 days. Later on, King Pimpolius added two months, Jonu Arius and Februarius to it and made it 12 months with 355 days, but in later years, because of the movement of the planets, the difference kept on increasing. Then, in 46 BC, Julius Caesar ordered a new calendar which had 365¼ days so as to set the difference right. That is why, in history, year 46 BC is known as the 'Year of Confusion'.

JULIAN CALENDAR

Caesar gave 365¼ days to a year. Serially, the months were given 31 and 30 days. February had 29 days, but in a leap year, it had 30 days. Along with this, to immortalise his name, he changed the name of the seventh month from its old name Quinitiles to July, which had, and still has 31 days. Later on came Emperor Augustus, who changed the name of the eighth month from Sextilis to August, to immortalise his name. At that time, August had 30 days but, to show that he was as great as Caesar, he took one day off from February, which contained 29 days then, and added it to August. Since then, the days and the months have continued to remain the same.

GREGORIAN CALENDAR

In the 16th century, the Julian calendar was increased by 10 days and the church festivals like Easter etc started getting into trouble. So, Pope Gregory XIII issued an order in1582 to rectify it by observing 4th October as 15th October and the beginning of the year from January 1 instead of March 25. The Roman Catholics accepted the order of the Pope with immediate effect but the Protestants took some time to accept it. Britain kept following the Julian Calendar and by 1752, there was a difference of 11 days. Hence, to rectify it, the day after September 2 was observed as 14th September. At that time, people used to shout slogans of **"Criseus back our 11 days."** After England, Bulgaria accepted the Gregorian Calendar in 1918 and then, in 1924, the Greek Orthodox Church also adopted it.

HISTORY OF MEASUREMENT OF TIME IN INDIA

India had the tradition of studying minute planetary movements. Calculations continued to be made on the basis of the movements of the earth, moon and the sun. To bridge the difference in the motion of the sun and the moon, there has been a practice of adding an extra month (*Adhik maas*). The various units of time and their reasons have been described below in brief:

Day[2] **-** *Saawan* day – The earth rotates on its axis at a speed of 1600 km per hour. To complete one rotation, it takes 24 hours. That part of the earth which stays in front of the sun for 12 hours has been called ***Ahah*** and the part that is behind, has been called ***Raatr***. This way, there are 24 ***horas*** in one ***ahoraatra***. It seems as if the word 'hour' in the English language is the slang form of the *hora*. *Saawan din* has been called ***Bhoo din*** (Earth Day).

Saur* day -** The earth is going around the sun at a speed of 1 lakh km per hour. A one degree movement of the earth is called a ***Saur din (Solar Day).

***Chandra Din* or *tithi* -** A Chandra din or lunar day has been called a *tithi*, for exampie *Ekam, Chaturthi, Ekadashi, Purnima, Amavasya, etc.*The movement of the moon to the twelfth part, while going around the earth, is called a *tithi*.

***Saptaah* (Week)**[3] **-** The days of the week and their sequence throughout the world are the same as has been discovered in India. The sequence of the planets was determined as per their progressive distances from the earth. Hence, Saturn, Jupiter, Mars, Sun, Venus, Mercury and Moon. Of these, the moon is the closest to the earth and Saturn is the farthest. Each planet is the ruler for one hour out of the 24 hours or *hora* day. Hence, each of the seven planets become the ruler for one hour by turn. This cycle goes on and once the 24 hours are complete, the name of the next day is according to the planet that is the ruler in the first hour of that day. Since creation started with the sun, hence the first day of the week was Sunday and the other days were named sequentially.

We can easily understand the sequence of the seven days as per the table given below:

Moon	Mercury	Venus	Sun	Mars	Jupiter	Saturn
4	3	2	Sunday 1	–	–	–
11	10	9	8	7	6	5
18	17	16	15	14	13	12
Mon 1	24	23	22	21	20	19
8	7	6	5	4	3	2
15	14	13	12	11	10	9
22	21	20	19	18	17	16
5	4	3	2	Tues 1	24	23
12	11	10	9	8	7	6
19	18	17	18	15	14	13
2	Wed 1	24	23	22	21	20
9	8	7	6	5	4	3
16	15	14	13	12	11	10
23	22	21	20	19	18	17
6	5	4	3	2	Thurs 1	24
13	12	11	10	9	8	7
20	19	18	17	16	15	14
3	2	Fri 1	24	23	22	21
10	9	8	7	6	5	4
17	16	15	14	13	12	11
24	23	22	21	20	19	18
						Satur 1

Fortnight–When the moon, while going around the earth, moves 12 degrees it is known as a *tithi*. On the new moon night (*amavasya)*, the moon lies between the sun and the earth. This is called zero degree. When the moon moves 12 parts and is at a distance of 180 degrees from the sun, it is called full moon (*Poornima)*. The fortnight from the first day after *amavasya* to *poornima* is called the *shukla paksh* and the fortnight from poornima to amavasya is called *krishna paksh*.

Month[4]**–**For the purpose of calculations, 27 constellations (*nakshatras*) have been accepted:

1. *Ashwini*
2. Bharani
3. Krittika
4. Rohini
5. Mrigashira
6. Aardra
7. Punarvasu
8. Pushya
9. Ashlesha
10. Magha
11. Poorva Phalgun
12. Uttar Phalgun
13. Hast
14. Chitra
15. Swati
16. Vishakha
17. Anuradha
18. Jyeshtha
19. Mool
20. Poorvasharh
21. Uttarasharh
22. Shravana
23. Dhanishtha
24. Shatabhishak
25. Poorva Bhadrapad
26. Uttar Bhadrapad
27. Revati

Each of the 27 constellations were divided into 4 quadrants thus there is a total of 108 quadrants. According to the shapes of 9 of these quadrants, the 12 zodiac signs were given their names:

1. Aries
2. Taurus
3. Gemini
4. Cancer
5. Leo
6. Virgo
7. Libra
8. Scorpio
9. Sagittarius
10. Capricorn
11. Aquarius
12. Pisces

The lines of these signs on earth were determined. It was called kranti. The lines are believed to be 24° north and south of the equator. Hence, the name of the sign which the sun reaches during the rotation of the earth is given to that solar month. These months generally neither increase nor decrease.

Lunar Month - The lunar months got their names from the star (*nakshatra*) that is visible throughout the month from evening to morning and in which the moon acquires completeness:

1. Chitra
2. Vishaakhaa
3. Jyeshtha
4. Ashaadhaa
5. Shravan
6. Bhaadrapad
7. Ashwini
8. Krittika
9. Mrigashira
10. Pushya
11. Magha
12. Phalguni

Hence, on this basis, the months were named *Chaitra, Vaishakha, Jyeshtha, Aashadha,Shraavan, Bhaadrapad, Ashwin, Kartika, Maargasheersha, Paush, Maagh* and *Phalgun.*

Summer solstice and winter solstice[5] - The earth is tilted 23½° north–westward on its axis. Therefore, 23½° north and south of the equator are the places, where the sun's rays fall vertically. This is called *Sankranti.* The line which is 23½° North is called the Tropic of Cancer or *Kark rekha* and 23½° South is called the Tropic of Capricorn or *Makar rekha.* The line with 0° (the equator) is called the *vishuv vritt rekha.* The *Kark Sankranti* is called *uttaraayan* or summer solstice and *Makar Sankranti* is called *dakshinaayan* or winter solstice.

Measure of a Year[6] - At a speed of about one lakh km per hour, the earth completes one revolution around the 966,000,000 kms path of the sun in 365½ days. This period is considered to be one year.

Measure of an Age[7] - In 432,000 years, all the seven planets leave their Longitude and Latitude and collect in one place. The time of this conjuncture is *kaliyug.* When two conjunctures take place it is *dwaapar,* when three take place, it is *treta* and when four conjunctures take place, it is called *satyug*. In the *chaturyugi*, all the seven planets, along with their Longitude and Latitude, lie in one direction only.

The present *kaliyug*, according to Indian calculations, started 3102 years BC, on the 20th of February at 2 hours, 27 minutes and 30 seconds. At that time, all the planets were under one zodiac sign. In this context, it is worth making a note of what Bally, the famous astronomer of Europe, has to say:

"According to the planetary calculations of the Hindus, the present age, that is *kaliyug*, started 3,102 years ago on the 20th of February at 2 hours 27 minutes and 30 seconds. As such, these calculations were made even to the second. The Hindus further say that all the planets were under the same zodiac sign at the time of *kaliyug* and their tables also say so. The calculations made by the Brahmins prove absolutely correct according to our astronomical tables. This is only because the results have been obtained by direct observation of the planets."[8]

(*Theogony of Hindus* by Bjornstjerna, Page 32)

According to the Vedic sages, the present universe is made of five *mandals* (orbits) - the moon orbit, earth orbit, sun orbit, *parameshthi mandal* and the *swayambhu mandal*. They are progressively moving round the higher orbits.

Manvantara[9] - The time that the sun takes to complete one orbit of the centre of the Milky Way (*Parameshthi mandal*) has been called a *manvantara*. It measures 30,67,20,000 (30 crore 67 lakh 20 thousand) years. The difference between two *Manvantaras* (*sandhyaansh*) is equal to one *satyug*. Therefore, the measurement of one *manvantar* along with its *sandhyaansh* is 30 crore 84 lakh 48 thousand years. According to modern measurements, the sun completes one orbit of the centre of the Milky Way in 25-27 crore years.

Era[10] – The *parameshthi mandal* is going round the *swayambhu mandal*. This means that our Milky Way is going round the Milky Way above it. The period it takes to do that has been called an era (*kalpa*) and measures 4 billion 32 million years (4320,000,000). This has been called one day of Brahma. The day is as long as the night. Hence, Brahma's *ahoraatra* is 864 crore years and Brahma's year is 31 *kharab 10 arab 40 crore* years. Brahma's age is 100 years. Therefore, the age of the universe is 31 *neel 10 kharab 40 arab* years (31,10,40000000000 years).

Studying the calculations of the Indians, Carl Segan, the famous Cosmologist of Europe has, in his book *Cosmos* said, "The Hindu religion is the only one which is dedicated to the belief that a particular sequence of the creation and destruction of the universe is going on and this is the only religion which has made calculations from the ordinary day and night to Brahma's day and night of 8 arab 64 crore years which, by coincidence, is close to the modern astronomical calculations. This calculation is older than the age of the earth and the sun. Besides, they possess measures for even larger calculations."[11] Carl Segan has called it a 'coincidence' but in fact it is based on solid planetary calculations.

AMAZING DISCOVERY OF THE SAGES

Our ancestors not only measured time on the basis of astronomical movements, they also formulated an amazing system to join the unending journey of time to the present and for the common man to know about it. We do not generally pay attention to it. In our country, we perform some religious procedures or ceremonies before doing any work—whether it be the beginning of manufacturing something, entry into a new house, birth, marriage or any other work. For this, one first has to take a *Sankalp* (resolution). The *Sankalp mantra* tells us about the state of time from ancient times to the present. So, if we concentrate on the meaning of the mantra, everything becomes clear.

In the *Sankalp mantra,* we say

> ***Om asya shri vishnoraagyayaa pravartamaanasya Brhmanaam dwiteeye paraardhe***

The mantra means that in the unending wheel of time pioneered by Maha Vishnu, the age of the present Brahma has completed 50 years. ***Shweta varaah kalpe-kalpa*** means that it is the first day of the 51st year of Brahma.

Vaivasvatamanvantare – There are 14 *manvantaras* in one day of Brahma. The 7th of these is the *vaivasvat manvantara,* which is going on.

Ashtaavinshatitame Kaliyuge – There are 71 *chaturyugis* in one *manvantar.* Of these, the *kaliyug* of the 28th chaturyugi is going on nowadays.

Kaliyuge Prathamacharane - The beginning of the *kaliyug.*

Kalisamvate or ***Yugaabde*** – At present, the *kalisamvat* or *yugaabd* is 5108 (2006 AD).

Jambu dweepe, Brahmaavarta deshe, Bhaarat khande – names of continents, region and country.

In such and such place – Place of work.

In such and such *samvatsar* – Name of the *samvatsar.*

In such and such *ayane* – *uttaraayan* or *dakshinaayan.*

In such and such *ritu* or season – There are six seasons including the spring season.

In such and such month – There are 12 months like *Chaitra* etc.

In such and such *paksh* or fortnight – Name of the fortnight as in *Shukla paksh* or *Krishna paksh.*

On such and such date or *tithi* – Name of the *tithi.*

On such and such day – Name of the day.

At such and such time – At what time of the day.

Such and such person – You take your name, then your father's name, then *gotra* and what work you are going to do and with what purpose – And then, you do the *sankalpa*.

It is with this system that remembering time from the time the *sankalp* is taken to eternity, has been easily brought into normal practice in the Indian way of life.

RELATIVITY OF TIME

Einstein established the relativity of time in his 'Theory of Relativity'. He said that the concept of time on the various planets varies. Time is related to the movement of the planet. Hence, the measurement of time on various planets is different.

Time is large and small. We get indications of this in our scriptures. There is a story in the Puranas that Rewati, the daughter of King Raiwatak, was very tall. So, it was difficult to find a suitable bridegroom for her. For a solution, the king took her to *Brahmalok* with the power of yoga. When he reached there, a *Gandharva gaan* was going on. So, he waited for some time. When the gaan was over, Brahma saw the king and asked him how he had come there? The king asked him if he had made any groom for his daughter. Brahma laughed out aloud and said, "While your were here, listening to the *gaan*, 27 *chaturyugis* have already passed on earth and the 28th, *dwaapar*, is about to finish. Go back and marry her off to Balaram, the brother of Krishna. He also said that it was good that he had brought Rewati with him because now, she had not grown older. This story shows the difference in time if one goes at great speed from the earth to *Brahmalok*. Even the modern scientists have said that if a person travels in a vehicle which runs at a speed a little less than light, then the process of ageing will be virtually still. If a 10-year-old human being goes in such a vehicle to the Andromeida Galaxy and returns, then his age will increase by only 56 years, whereas 40 lakh years will have elapsed on earth during that period.[12]

In the *Yogavashishtha* and other scriptures, one finds descriptions of going back into time and experiencing previous births and going into the future too, through *yoga sadhana.*

In this context, George Gemov of the western world has written an interesting poem in his book *One, Two, Three, Infinity*:

> "There was a young girl named Miss Bright
> Who could travel much faster than light
> She departed one day
> In an Einstein way
> And came back on the previous night."[13]

□

12

Astronomy

Astronomy was called 'the eyes of the *Vedas*', because the behaviour of all creations is determined by time and time is known through the movement of the planets. Hence, astronomy has been a part of the *Vedas* and *Vedanga* since ancient times. We find innumerable examples in the *Rigveda, Shatpath, Brahmin* and the other books about the stars, the lunar and solar months, the extra month, changes in seasons, the significance of the sun, unit of era (*kalpa*) etc. The sages carried out direct observations for this purpose. It is said that Sage Deerghatamas became blind while studying and observing the sun. Sage Gritsmad spoke about the effects of the moon on the foetus. In the 40th mantra of the 18th chapter of the *Yajurveda,* it is said that the moon shines because of the rays of the sun.

There was a method to use machines for astronomical observations. More than 1500 years ago, during the time of Aryabhatta, there was an observatory in Pataliputra where Aryabhatta drew many conclusions after observing the sky.

In the chapter on machines in the book *Siddhanta*

Shiromani, Bhaskaracharya says, "It is not possible to gain knowledge of the small fractions of time without the help of machines." He describes the *naadivalay yantra, yashti yantra, ghati yantra, chakra yantra, shanku yantra, chaap, turya, phalak etc.*[1]

The history of direct observation and accurate/exact calculations of time and planets is more than 6000 year old[2]:

In his book *Indian Science and Technology in the Eighteenth Century*, Shri Dharmapalji has published an article entitled 'Remarks on the Astronomy of the Brahmins' by the famous astronomer, John Playfair (published in 1790). This article proves that India had knowledge in astronomy for more than 6000 years and that Indian calculations were applied throughout the world. The article says that in 1687, M.L. Labbett, who was in the French embassy in Siam, brought a calendar with him to France. Missionaries had sent two calendars from India – one from south India and one from Varanasi. Likewise, M.D. Lisle sent another calendar, which was from Narasaapur in south India. The French mathematicians of the time could not understand these calendars. So, they sent them to John Playfair, who was the Royal Astronomer at that time. When he started studying them, he realised that although they were from different places the principle on which they had been made, was the same.

Another amazing thing that came to Playfair's notice was that the Meridian given in the Siamese calendar was 18° (degrees) – 15′ (minutes) West, but Siam was not situated on this Meridian. It was surprising that it joined the Meridian of Varanasi. This meant that the basis of the Siamese calendar was also India.

The second thing that he says, all the calendars speak of the same year – which they consider the beginning of kaliyug and of the position of the stars as they were on the first few days of *kaliyug*. They calculate the time also accordingly. They tell us what the position of the planets was at that time. It seems strange because *kaliyug* is believed to have started around 3000 BC. It seems strange, that the positions of Jupiter, Saturn, Mars, Mercury, Venus, etc. had been written about so long ago. After analysing it in great detail, Playfair says, "There is striking similarity between the position of the planets as given in the ancient calendars and those that have been prepared with the help of the modern methods available today." Playfair gives two alternatives as to how this could be possible.

1. The Brahmins must have developed a flawless and accurate way of counting. They were already well acquainted with the rules of the universe's gravitation to attract the distant and near planets.
2. The Brahmins had observed the sky in a scientific way.

Playfair selects the second alternative and accepts that the Brahmins had, in the past, observed and studied the sky clearly. The calendars they made in the past with ordinary means, are amazing. They used geography, arithmetic and trigonometry to prepare them.

In the end, Playfair says two things:

1. This proves that astronomy was studied in India from 3000 BC and that the position of the sun and the moon, at the time of the beginning of *kaliyug*, as described, was based on actual observations.
2. It must have taken 1000-1200 years to develop and propagate such a pure knowledge. Hence, we can say that in 4300 BC, astronomy was developed in India on the basis of direct experiences.

The analysis of a neutral foreigner inspires us to act further.

Shri Dharmpalji has, in this book, written that Sir Robert Barker, the Commander-in-Chief of the British Army in contemporary Bengal, who later became a member of the British Parliament, had, in 1777, thrown light on an ancient Indian Observatory in an article entitled 'Brahmin Observatory in Benaras'. In 1772, he had examined the observatory. At that time, it was in a dilapidated state as it had not been used for a long time. Even so, the machines and means that were left were studied minutely by Barker. An important thing that struck him was that these things had been made about 400 years ago. Their measurements, their calculations, etc. were all flawless.

GLIMPSES OF ANCIENT ASTRONOMY

1. **Speed of light** – Did our ancestors have any knowledge about the speed of light? Shri K.K. Shah, Governor of Gujarat had once asked this question to Prof. L Shivayya, Lecturer of Physics at Mysore University. Shri Shivayya was knowledgeable in both Science and Sanskrit. He immediately replied, "Yes, they did" and, as a proof, he told him of the two *richas* in the first part of the *Rigveda*.

   Mano na yoadhvanah sadya etyekah satraa sooro vasva eeshe

   'Like the mind, the sun that moves on the heavenly path all alone." (*Rig*. 1-71-9)

   Taranirvishwadarshato jyotikridasi soorya vishwamaabhasirochanam

"O Sun! You move with great speed and are extremely good looking, you give light to the world." (*Rig*. 1.50.9)

In a commentary on thses *richas,* while describing the speed of the sun, Saganacharya writes a *shloka* which talks about the speed of light.

Yojananaam sahastre dwe dweshate dwe cha yojane
Eken nimishaardhena kramamaan namoastu te[3]

"Salutations to you, O Light ! that travels 2202 *yojans* in half *nimesh.*"

In this, 1 *yojan* = 9 miles 160 yards
Which means 1 *yojan* = 9.11 miles
1 day-night has 810000 half *nimesh*
Hence, 1 second = 9.41 half *nimesh*
In this way 2202 × 9.11 = 20060.22 miles per half *nimesh*
And 20060.22 × 9.41 = 188766.67 miles per second
This is very close to the speed of light acceptable to the modern science.

2. **Gravitational Pull–** "Father, the earth on which we live, rests on which thing?"
Leelavati had asked this question hundreds of years ago to her father, Bhaskaracharya. In reply, Bhaskaracharya said, "O daughter, Leelavati ! Those people who say that the earth is resting on the *sheshnaag* (cobra snake), the tortoise or elephant or any other thing, are wrong. If we accept that it is based on something, then the question that arises is, that thing rests on which thing? Thus, the reason and its reason…if this sequence continues, then it

is known as a state of uncondition in jurisprudence."

Leelavati still insisted on asking the question.

Then, Bhaskaracharya said, "Why can we not accept that the earth is not based on anything? What is wrong in saying that the earth is standing on its own strength and call it its power of retention?"

At this Leelavati asked how it was possible?

Then, Bhaskaracharya speaks of principles and says that the power of things is very peculiar[4]

Marucchalo bhoorachala swabhaawato yato
Vichitravatavastu shaktyah

– (*Siddhant Shiromani Golaadhyay-Bhuvankosh* –5)

He further says:

Aakrishtishaktishch mahi taya yat khastham
Guru swabhimukham swashaktya.
Aakrishyate tatpatateev bhaati
Samesamantaat kwa patatviyam khe.

– (*Siddhanta Shiromani Golaadhyay-Bhuvankosh* –6)

This means that the earth has the power of attraction. So, it attracts heavy things towards itself and because of the attraction, they fall to the ground. But, when an equal power or strength pulls from all directions in the sky, then how can a thing fall? This means that the planets stay in the sky without any support because the gravitational powers of the various planets maintain the balance.

Today, we say that Newton was the first to discover the gravitational power of the earth, but 550 years before him, Bhaskaracharya had spoken about it.

3. **The Earth is Round -** Leelavati asks her father how he can say that the earth is round when she can see only a flat surface all around?

Bhaskaracharya says that what we see is not always the truth. He says that if you draw a large circle and look at only a hundredth part of its circumference, then it will appear to be a straight line; but actually it is not so. It is curved. Similarly, we see only a small part of the sphere of this huge earth. Hence, it seems flat to us. In reality, the earth is round.[5]

Indian Model of Earth (on Bronze) with Stars shown in Silver (1600 AD).

Samo yatah syaatparidheh shataanshah
Prithvi cha prithvi nitaraam taneeyaan
Narashcha tatprishthagatasya kritsnaa
Sameva tasya pratibhaatyatah saa.

– (Siddhanta Shiromani golaadhyay-Bhuvankosh 13)

4. **The Earth is not Stationary -** Till Galileo's time in the 15th century in the west, people believed that the earth was stationary and that the sun revolved around the earth. But 1500 years ago, Aryabhatta

had stated that the earth moves on its axis, in the following way:

Anulomagatirnausthah pashyatyachalam
Vilomagam yadvat.
Achalaani bhaani tadvat sama
Pashchimagaani lankaayaam.

— (*Aryabhattiya Golapaad–9*)

Just as a person travelling in a boat feels that the rocks, trees, etc. (which are otherwise stationary) are moving in the opposite direction, similarly, the stars seem to be moving from east to west.
Prithudak Swami, who has written a commentary on Brahmagupta's principle of the Brahmasphut, has also mentioned an *aarya* of Aryabhatta.

Bha panjarah sthiro bhoo rewaavrityaavritya praati daivasikau
Udayaastamayau sampaadayati nakshatragrahaanaam.[6]

It means that the constellation is stationary and the earth, with its movement, appears to make the planets and stars rise and set.
In the *Dashageetika* chapter of his book, *Aryabhattiya*, Aryabhatta has clearly written ***Praane naiti kalaam bhooh*** which means that in one *praan*, the earth rotates one degree. (There are 21,600 *praans* in one day)

5. **Sunrise – Sunset** – Because the earth is spherical and because there is a difference in the longitudes of various cities, sunrise and sunset take place at different times in different places. Aryabhatta had realised this. That is why, he writes,

Udayo yo Lankaayaam sostamayah
Savitureva Siddhapure.
Madhyanho yavakotyaam romaka
Vishayeardharatrah syaat.

— *(Aryabhattiya Golapaad –13)*

"When the sun rises in Lanka, it sets in Siddhapur; it is afternoon in Yavakoti and midnight in Cilia."

6. **Solar and Lunar Eclipse –** Aryabhatta said that an eclipse occurs because of the shadow of the moon on the earth and not because of *Rahu* and *Ketu*.

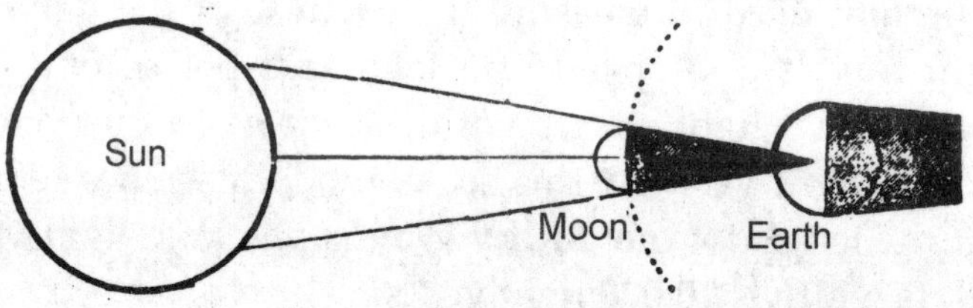

Solar eclipse

Chhadayati shashi suryam mahatich bhuchchhaya (Aryabhattiya-37)

That is, when the massive shadow of the earth falls on the moon, it leads to a lunar eclipse. Similarly, when the moon comes between the earth and the sun, a solar eclipse occurs.

7. **Distance of the various planets**[7] – Aryabhatta has also written about the distances of the various planets from the sun. It is very much similar to the modern measurements. Today, the sun is at a distance of **1.5×10^8 kms** = 15 crore kms from the earth. It is called **AU** or Astronomical Unit. On the basis of this

proportion, we can make the following list:

Planet	Aryabhatta's measurement	Today's measurement
Mercury	0.375 AU	0.387 AU
Venus	0.725 AU	0.723 AU
Mars	1.538 AU	1.523 AU
Jupiter	5.16 AU	5.20 AU
Saturn	9.41 AU	9.54 AU

Expanse of the Universe: Our ancestors had also experienced the expanse of the universe. Today, light year is the unit used to measure the expanse of the universe. Light travels at a speed of 3 lakh kms per second. The distance that light covers with this speed in one year, is called a light year. At this scale, modern science tells us that the length of our **Milky Way** is one lakh light years and its width is 10,000 light years.

The **Androlla Milky Way,**which is above our Milky Way, is at a distance of 20 lakh 20,000 light years and there are crores of such milky ways in the universe.

In the *Shrimad Bhagwat,* King Pareekshit asks Sage Shukdev what the extent of the universe is? With this reference, Shukdev says that a mantle ten-fold the size of our universe, is covering it. Each mantle is ten times bigger than the previous one and there are seven such mantles that he knew of. In all these, the entire universe seems like an atom. There are crores of such universes. This is the reason of all reasons[8]. This seems a little unimaginable to the mind. But, the one supreme power, whom we believe to be the Creator, of the innumerable names that He is believed to have, one is ***Anant Koti Brahmaanda Naayak.*** Whereas this name speaks of the infinity of the universe, it also gives the feeling of being scientific.

Thus, through this brief observation, we can say that India has had a glorious tradition of astronomy and the calculation of time. During the last few centuries, this idea has been somewhat impeded. The teachers of the ancient times are inspiring today's generation to take it forward.

□

13

Architecture

The sphere of our architectural science has been quite comprehensive. It included town planning, buildings, temples, sculpting, fine arts and literally everything. Roads, water supply systems, public bathrooms, drains, different shapes and kinds of buildings, their directions, measurement, land – types of land, nature of materials used for constructions, etc. were contemplated upon in great details in town planning. It was also seen that these were all nature-friendly. Dams, wells, streams, rivers were also considered among water-supply systems.

How minutely and in what detail they studied such things even thousands of years ago!

Mud, bricks, lime, stone, wood, metal, gems, etc. were used for architecture. It was said that each item must be examined thoroughly and used according to its necessity, in construction. We get an idea of how scientific were the measures used to examine each item from the following example:

Sage Bhrigu says that each item used in construction

should be tested as per the following criteria:

> ***Varnalingavayovasthah parokshyam cha balabalam***
> ***Yathayogyam, yathashaktih Sanskarankarayet Sudheeh.***
>
> – *(Bhrigu Samhita)*

He stresses that all traditions must consider the chroma (colour), gender (property, mark), age (from time of implant till date) condition, along with its strength or weakness and the force that will be exerted on them.[1]

Here chroma means colour. But in architecture, colour is used in accordance with its power to reflect light, e.g. white colour reflects light completely. It is, therefore, said to be an excellent colour.

In the context of construction, a number of books by sages of ancient times, are available such as:

1. ***Vishwakarma Vastushastra*:** The first thing that Vishwakarma tells us about construction is **"Poorva – bhoomim parikshyet pashchat vaastu prakalpayet"** that is, one must first test the land and then start construction there. Vishwakarma further says that one must not construct anything on such a land, which is very rocky, which is hilly, where there are a large number of cracks or crevices, etc.
2. ***Kashyap Shilp*:** Sage Kashyap says that a foundation should be dug till the water is seen because after that there are rocks.
3. ***Bhrigu Samhita*:** In this, Bhrigu says that before buying land, it must be tested in five different ways, i.e. appearance, colour, taste, smell and touch. He also tells how to do it.

For the construction of a building, he has given a detailed description of the walls, their thickness and the internal arrangements, etc.

The ruins of constructions carried out on the basis of this knowledge still exist even after centuries. Some examples are as follows:

Mohanjodaro (Sind)[2] **–** The archeological excavations reveal the amazing construction of this wonderful city that dates back to 3000 BC. It was an extremely well-planned city whose houses, roads, etc. had all been made as per geometrical measurements. The roads found here were absolutely straight, running from east to west and from north to south. The other amazing thing is that they crossed one-another at an angle of 90 degrees.

Houses were made in the right proportions; the joints of bricks and the heights of walls were equal. There were arrangements for dining room, bathroom and bed room, etc. Besides residential houses, lawns, public places for various programmes, a massive public bathroom is also found which is 11.89 metres long, 7.01 metres wide and 2.44 metres high with two streams of water feeding it. Secondly, the walls were made of something which would remain unaffected by water. Observing this, one feels that those who had built this city must have been very well versed in architectural science.

Dwarka – Dr. S.R. Rao discovered Dwarka during archeological excavations. The ancient traces or ruins that have been found there tell us that Dwarka too, was a well planned city surrounded by a wall. The buildings were made of a stone that would not corrode in sea water. One can see double-storeyed buildings, roads and water arrangements. Copper, brass and some mixed metals have also been found. The mixed metals had 34 per cent zinc. The measurements and shapes of pillars, window panes, etc. used for the buildings, were all calculated mathematically.

Lothal Port (Saurashtra)[3] **-** The port at Lothal was built around 2500 BC where not just small barges, but even big ships took harbour. Because of the port, a big city had also developed here. Its construction was very similar to that of Mohanjodaro and Harappa. Roads, buildings, gardens, lawns and public buildings were all there. The cremation ground was built a little away from the city dwelling.

Lothal Port was spread 300 metres north-south and 400 metres east-west. It had a 13 metres high wall, made of mud, bricks etc. to keep floods and storms away. This port was far more developed than the Fonetian and Roman ports made later.

Varanasi[4] **-** Claud Wetley has observed that India's great architectural heritage has been neglected or disregarded. Many of the modern buildings, despite their magnificence, are unfavourable due to India's climate, its monsoon winds, rain, water and the perpendicular rays of the sun.

Stone chairs, thick walls, windows slanting towards the floors so that there was free circulation of air, inner courtyards, basements and the construction of a terrace-shaped thatched roof were all prevalent according to India's traditional architecture. All these things were taken into consideration for the convenience of the community and better health. Varanasi has been accepted or acknowledged as the first organised city of the world. Prof. Bhim Chandra Chatterjee, scholar of hydro-power engineering in ancient India, writes that four generations of Ayodhya's rulers had devoted their lives to bring the river Ganga from the Himalayas, but finally, the great Bhagirath succeeded. The flow of the Ganga was redirected towards the Bay of Bengal. At Varanasi, it seems to turn towards the north and branches out into two - *Varun* and *Asi*, both fed by the Ganga, as they are derived from it. At places where the intensity of water is very high, the excess water can be made to flow out. There is no other example to show such a brilliant way of preventing floods.

Nine important things about city planning (*navagam nagaram prahuh*)[5]–

1. **Water Supply :** Drinking water, purification of water and sewage.
2. **Waiting Rooms:** Rest rooms for travellers, *dharmashalas*, guest houses.
3. **Markets:** Place for buying and selling consumer items.
4. **Penal and Crime Investigation by Police:** System of legislation of punishment, Law and order and safety from anarchical elements.
5. **Horticulture:** For parks, merriment and pleasure, and for educational institutions.
6. **Population:** Residential system, workshops, factories.
7. **Crematorium:** Burning grounds and arrangement for dispersal of ashes.
8. **Health:** Hospitals and centres for health diagnosis.
9. **Temples:** Place for Gods and Goddesses, conveniences for the followers of all the faiths, caste or creed, places for intercourses and public celebrations.

RARE EXAMPLE OF CITY PLANNING IN ANCIENT INDIA[6]

Kanjivaram is an excellent example of city planning. Town planners all over the world are amazed at the planning of Kanjivaram.

Writing about the prominent grandeur in the town planning in the South in ancient India, C.P.Venkatram Aiyyar says in 1916 that the ancient town of Kanjivaram is a rare example of the excellent traditional town planning. Prof. Gadade has called it an excellent example of public thinking on town planning and has praised it a lot. The astute planning, to assure complete comfort has impressed Prof. Gadade immensely. It is solid proof of town planning in ancient India. According to him, the architects have shown how high and how excellent public thinking can be. They have beautified this city of temples with their imagination. Temples not merely impart a beautiful image to the town, but enrich it in many minute details that gives joy to one and all. The dreams of the various cults are realised here. The glory of human imagination and behaviour takes a tangible form here. At the same time, an artist enjoys personal and artistic autonomy as well. This is not possible anywhere else in the world even in the most prosperous cities.

Circumstances opposite to this can be seen from St. Andrews to Eden, Lincoln to New York, Oxford to Salisbury, Excella Chapele to Cologne and Freeburg Robor to Nimes. There is a complete lack of feeling about town planning. They are settlements of huts. To be free of all these distortions is a proof of excellent quality of Indian architecture and enriched town planning.

Management of Water Supply - We get amazing examples of water supply systems from 2500-3000 BC to the 17th century AD in various parts of the country. These include big ponds, streams and channels to get water from other areas into the towns.

One amazing example - The most amazing example is of the channelising of the flow of the Ganga by Bhagirath. In ancient times, the area towards Tibet was known as Heaven. Hence, when the Pandavas went for *swargarohan,* their path led from the Himalayas to Tibet. According to the Puranas, the river Ganga previously flowed in heaven.

It was King Bhagirath who changed its course and brought it down to our country from heaven. Referring to this, Sir William Wilcolmes had, in his speech on 'Ancient Irrigation Systems and the Present Problems' at Calcutta University in 1935, said,

"Seventy-seven years ago, I was born in a tent that had been put up for irrigation and I spent my entire life in irrigation work and in drenching the country. According to the *Mahabharata*, Bhagirath brought the Ganga down and regulated it. The amazingly brilliant writers of the ancient times expressed this truth at great length in spiritual language, but the facts are the same. Every canal that faced south, whether it was the Bhagirathi or the Mathbhanga canal, is basically a canal only. They were all dug out parallel to each other and were therefore similar. They were made in such a way and at such a distance that one can understand the validity of the gap between the canals."[7]

Sir William Wilcolmes adds that when he was analysing the canal system of the country, he was amazed to see that the river that was considered dead in the map, seemed to have been converted into a canal.

Importance of water conservation – In his *Arthashastra* written 2500 years ago, Kautilya says that a king should try to store and save water with the same pious feeling that he has when he builds a temple. Today, there is a hue and cry over water. People fear that water may be the cause of the Third World War. At such a time, what Chanakya (Kautilya) said ought to be contemplated upon. Chanakya did not stop by only advising the king to make an effort to save water with pious feelings, he went further to say that a good king must inspire his people to conserve water. He must even provide financial assistance for this purpose and if need be, provide contributions to help his people in this work.

Kautilya even talks of building dams to store water. He says that a dam should not be built at a place where the borders of two states meet because if this happens, then it can be a cause for conflict. Today, when we see the controversies of the Cauvery and the Narmada rivers, one feels that he had great foresight.

Water Engineering in the South (Perumamil Reservoir)[8] - This reservoir was built in 1369 AD by Anantraja Sagar. It tells us the story of irrigation, architecture and technology. From the inscriptions dated 1369 AD, on the two rocks towards the temple nearby, we get to know that it took two years, 1000 labourers and 100 vehicles to carry the stones to the construction site, for building the reservoir. The inscription mentions 12 things that should be taken care of while selecting the site and starting the construction. These are considered necessary for the construction of a good pond.

1. The ruler must have a desire to earn a name by doing good deeds and working for the prosperity of his people.
2. He must be proficient in hydro sciences.
3. The base of the reservoir must be on solid ground.
4. The river must bring the water from about 38 km.
5. The dam must have mountain peaks on two sides.
6. The dam must be made of solid stone between these two mountains. It may not be long, but it must be solid.
7. These mountains must be different from the land which is fertile and good for cultivation.
8. The bed of the reservoir must be long, broad and deep.
9. The land must consist of straight and long stones.

10. Lower, fertile land should be available nearby for irrigation.
11. The base of the water force must be solid with stones.
12. Efficient workers must be employed to build the reservoir.

Six prohibitions or taboos are also carved on the rock inscriptions. These must be avoided at all cost.

1. Leakage from the dam.
2. Barren land.
3. Construction of the reservoir on the borders of two areas ruled by different people.
4. Raised area within the dam.
5. Induction of less water supply and larger areas for irrigation.
6. Insufficient land for irrigation and more water reservoirs.

Besides this, there are interesting historical records about the construction of structures for water conservation from the 11th century to the 17th century AD.

1. Structure of a temple along the Arikeshari Mangalam Reservoir 1010-11 AD.
2. The expanse of the dam, dome and canal of the Ganga Hakoda Cholpuram Reservoir (1012-1014 AD) is 16 miles.
3. The Bhojpur Lake (11th century AD), adjacent to Bhopal, is spread over 250 sq. miles. It had been constructed by King Bhoj, where 365 streams meet. The Bhopal lake is mentioned in sayings too. In fact, there is a Hindi idiom which says, ***"Taal ho to Bhopal taal, baaqi sab talaiya."***
4. Almanda Reservoir (11th century AD) in Vishakhapatnam.

5. Rajat Taaka Lake (11th century AD).
6. Bhavdev Bhatt Reservoir in Bengal.
7. Sindhughati Reservoir (1106-07 AD) was constructed in Mysore. The Periya Kyakkal Slues (1219 AD) is in District Trichilapalli.
8. Pakhala Jheel (13th century AD) is an example of the plough structure in District Warangal.
9. Phirangipuram Reservoir (1409 AD) in District Guntur, is an architectural masterpiece.
10. Haridra Reservoir (1410 AD) was constructed by the Brahmins at their own cost. At that time King Devraj was the ruler of Vijayanagar.
11. A mention of the Narsimha Vodhi Reservoir (1489 AD) in Anantpur District is also essential.
12. The Nagalpur Reservoir was constructed by King Krishnaraj in 1520 AD, to supply drinking water to the people of Nagalpur. Krishnaraj also has the honour of making the first underwater tunnel. This process came to be known as the Hindu underground channel. The construction of the Vijaypur, Mahmadnagar, Aurangabad, Koragaja, and Vasaganna channels are links in this chain.
13. Shivasamudra (1531-32 AD) is, even today, the source of water supply to Bangalore. A net of waterways is still present in north India, specially in Sind and Punjab.
14. Anangpal built the Tughlakabad dam in 1151 AD.
15. The Satpula dam in Delhi which was constructed in 1326 AD, has ***mehraabs*** which are 38 feet high.
16. The old canal of the Jamuna, which was called the Ferozeshah Tughlak Nahar (13th century AD), is built on the river Ravi.

ANCIENT TEMPLES - IMMORTAL EXAMPLES OF ARCHITECTURAL BEAUTY[9]

In ancient times, there were groups of artists who lived together as clans. If any royal or noble person or some rich man wanted to get a massive temple built, the artists would go there and with devotion and dedication, engage themselves in making idols and the temple without caring for any commercial gains. Their silent dedication would infuse life into the building. That is why, even today, the sculptures of the temples are so lively. The construction of the Sun Temple in Konark took 12 years, and is the result of the dedicated work of innumerable architects.

From this point of view, when one looks at the innumerable ancient buildings and temples, a thought comes in mind that the ancient artists kept the philosophy and tradition of India above everything else before selecting the holiest of places to build such massive monuments which are unsurpassable in the art of architecture. They sacrificed their entire lives to make these buildings which have stunned the human intellect. They broke up huge rocks and brought out white and red stones, chiselled them for days and created great works of art, without caring about hunger or thirst, and offered them as homage to their motherland. The public established their cultural and religious symbols in these massive buildings and spread the fame and glory of the artisans far and wide.

Many examples of this great art can be seen in various parts of the country. **The temples at Ellora**, of which the Brahmin temple Kailas is the biggest and the most beautiful, is an example of flawless and artistic architecture. It is 142 feet long, 62 feet wide and 100 feet high. Mythological scenes have been carved out on it.

The scene of the conversation between Shiv and Parvati seems to have been explicitly etched out by the craftsman in the **Elephanta Caves.**

The Lingaraj Temple of Orissa is an outstanding example of the art. The temple is built on an area of 520 × 465 sq. feet. Its height is 144.05 feet and is surrounded by a 7.5 foot thick wall. It has four main parts – Vimaan, Jagmohan, Nat mandir, and Bhaag Mandap. Besides the beautiful carvings of many Gods and Goddesses, many scenes from the *Ramayana* and the *Mahabharata* have also been carved out in the temple.

The temples at Khajuraho were built in the 9th century. Initially, there were 85 temples. Now, only about 20 remain. The temples of Khajuraho are a great symbol of architectural beauty. On the outer walls are the passionate postures and in the sanctum santorum there is a Shiv linga.

Besides these, the **temples of Girnar** in Gujarat are very famous. The **temple of Srirangapattan** is the biggest and an outstanding architectural example in the South. There is a *mandap* (16 × 70) with more than thousand pillars, and the room is 450 × 130 feet. The massive and artistic entrance, spiral creepers and floral engravings here create an absolutely amazing atmosphere.

The 11th century **Rameswaram** is one of the four places (*Dham*) of supreme pilgrimage.

The **Meenakshi temple at Madurai** is also an example of architectural beauty. It is 847 feet long, 795 feet broad and 160 feet high. Its boundary has 11 entrances. It also has a *mandap* of 1000 pillars. But its specialty is that on each of these pillars there are entirely different carvings of sculptures. This is the best example of the art of south India.

Throughout India, there are thousands of temples and palaces which tell the story of architectural knowledge in ancient times.

SOME MARVELLOUS EXAMPLES OF ARCHITECTURE

1. There is a statue of Lord Buddha in one of the caves of Ajanta which, if you look at from your left side, shows Buddha in a pensive mood; from the front, he seems to be contemplating deeply; and if you look at it from your right, he seems to be smiling. The expression on the face of the same statue changes if you look at it from different angles.
2. The Vitthal Mandir in the South, made during the Vijayanagar regime is an exquisite example of temple architecture. The musical aspect of this temple shows us the varieties of stone, and what special sound will be emitted from the stone if it is chiselled in a certain way and set up in a certain corner. One can actually feel the music and the instruments from the various pillars. There are seven pillars as you enter. If you place your ear on the first and hit it, the sound of 'sa' will be heard and in the same sequence, you can hear 're', 'ga', 'ma', 'pa', 'dha', 'ni' too. As you go further, you can hear the sounds of various musical instruments from the different pillars—you can hear the *tabla*, the *bansuri* (flute) and the *veena*. Those who carved this actually created music out of the stones. Even today, these immortal creations of those unknown and unsung artisans, tell the glorious saga of architecture.

THE ART OF PAINTING

The splendour and the beauty of the more than thousand year old paintings in the caves of Ajanta near Aurangabad in Maharashtra, are a subject of wonder for modern scholars. They depict incidents from the life of Gautam Buddha. They were made of colours prepared from a mixture of rice starch, gum, leaves and some other materials. They were underground for nearly a thousand years and were excavated and once again brought to light in 1819, yet neither their colours faded nor did they lose their lustre. All efforts to add fresh colour or renovate them failed. This technique of colour and lines reminds us, even today, of our glorious past.

Views of Mr. Griffith on the paintings of Ajanta caves - The British researcher, Mr. Griffith says, "The artists who did the paintings in Ajanta, were the topmost people in the world of creations. Even the straight vertical lines drawn with easy brush-strokes on the walls of Ajanta, are amazing. But when one looks at the lines drawn parallel to the horizon and the curves, sees the similarity and wonders at the thousand complexities of creation, it is felt that this is nothing short of a miracle."[10]

□

Chemistry

This science is related to metallurgy and medical science. In modern times, the famous scientist Acharya Prafulla Chandra Rai brought this forgotten science to the forefront by writing the book *Hindu Chemistry*. Chemistry is an experimental science. It helps in producing various compounds metals, and medicines for healthy living through minerals, plants and agricultural products.

There have been many Indian chemists in the past. The writings of some of them are as under:

Nagarjuna – *Rasratnakar, Kakshaputatantra, Arogya Manjari, Yog Saar, Yogashtak.*
Vagbhatta – *Ras Ratna Sammuchchay.*
Govindacharya – *Rasaarnav.*
Yashodhar – *Ras Prakash Sudhakar.*
Ramchandra – *Rasendra Chintamani.*
Somdev – *Rasendra Chudamani.*

The following chemicals are mentioned in the book *Ras Ratna Sammuchchay*[1]:

1. *Maharasa*
2. *Upras*
3. *Samanyaras*
4. *Ratna*
5. *Dhatu*
6. *Vish*
7. *Kshaar*
8. *Amal*
9. *Lavan*
10. *Lauhbhasma*

The **main chemicals** are:

1. *Abhram*
2. *Vaikrant*
3. *Bhashisk*
4. *Vimla*
5. *Shilajatu*
6. *Sasyak*
7. *Chapala*
8. *Rasak*

Upras:

1. *Gandhak*
2. *Gairik*
3. *Kashis*
4. *Suvari*
5. *Lalak*
6. *Manah Shila*
7. *Anjan*
8. *Kankushtha*

Samanya Ras:

1. *Koyila*
2. *Gauripaashaan*
3. *Navsaar*
4. *Varaatak*
5. *Agnijaar*
6. *Laajvarta*
7. *Giri Sindur*
8. *Hingul*
9. *Murdaad Shringakam*

Similarly, there are more than 10 ***vish*** (poison). There is a description of the acids as well. Solvent acids and all dissolving acids are also described.

Various kinds of ***alkalis*** and the ash of different metals are explained in these books.

LABORATORY[2]

A detailed description of a laboratory is given in chapter-7 of *Ras Ratna Samuchchay*. More than 32 instruments or apparatus were used here, the prominent among them are:

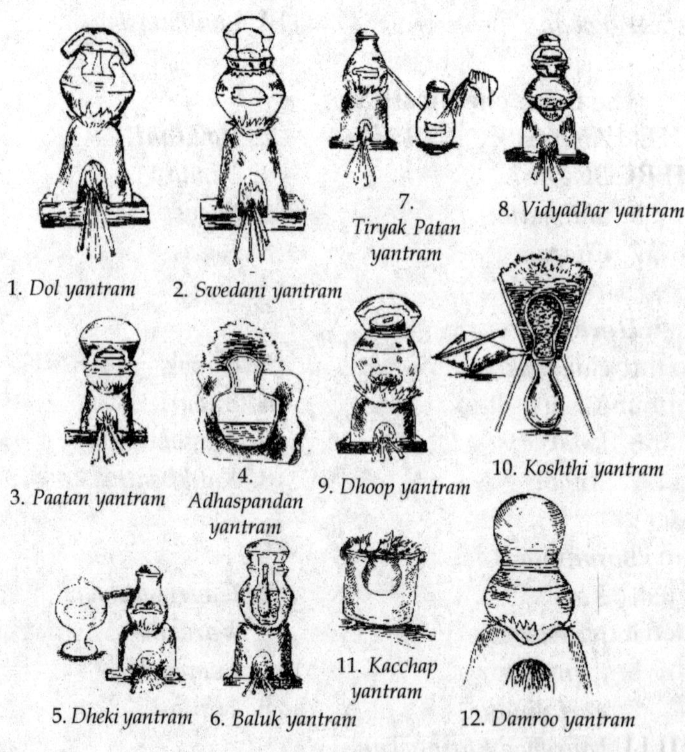

1. *Dol yantram* 2. *Swedani yantram* 3. *Paatan yantram* 4. *Adhaspandan yantram* 5. *Dheki yantram* 6. *Baluk yantram* 7. *Tiryak Patan yantram* 8. *Vidyadhar yantram* 9. *Dhoop yantram* 10. *Koshthi yantram* 11. *Kacchap yantram* 12. *Damroo yantram*

Nagarjuna carried out numerous experiments on mercury in the laboratory. He has explained in great detail how to purify mercury and how to use it for medicinal purposes. He has also given the methods of preparing mixtures of various metals, purifying mercury and other metals and the *maharasas* and how to convert metals into gold or silver.

Mercury is used not just in the conversion of a metal but also to make us disease-free and for longevity. The chemistry based on mercury is, in its fully developed form, linked to man-woman symbolism in India. Mercury is considered an element of Shiva, whereas sulphur, an element of Parvati[3] and the product that was created from their union in asafoetida was called *ras sindur,* which was considered the essence for longevity.

THE PROCESS FOR THE METAMORPHOSIS OF MERCURY[4]

From these books, realise that the scholars of chemistry knew the processes for the purification of minerals and metals, removing their harmful characteristics and making them suitable for internal consumption. Mercury had to go through 18 processes of purification. These included some prominent ones like combining it with the juices of medicinal plants and the mixing of mercury with sulphur, mica and some alkaline products. Scholars of chemistry believe that after going through the 17 processes of purification, mercury can change its form (into gold or silver) but all its powers must be tested or investigated. If it passes the final test, then it must be sent through the 18th process of purification. This way, mercury becomes fit for rejuvenation.

KILLING OR DESTROYING METALS

The method of destroying the qualities of metal in order to make it worthy of use, has also been described in these books. It was a common practice to destroy the metal in the laboratory. Sulphur was used to destroy all metals. Hence, in the book, sulphur has been compared to a lion and the other metals to an elephant. It is said that just as a lion kills an elephant, similarly, sulphur destroys all metals. Govindacharya, the Chemistry scholar says—

Naasti tallohamatango yanna gandhakakeshari
Nihanyadwandhamaatrena yadwa makshikakeshari.

– *(Rasarnava-7-138-142)*[5]

Conversion of zinc into gold: We all know that if one part of zinc is mixed with three parts of copper and heated, it changes into brass, which is a golden coloured mixture. Nagarjuna says –

Kramen kritwambudharen ranjitah
Karoti shulvam triputen kaanchanam

– *(Rasratnaakar-3)*[6]

The non-rusting ability of metals: Govindacharya has described, the sequence of the abilities of metals to fight rusting and corrosion. Even today, the same system is followed –

Suvarnam rajatam tamram teekshnavangam bhujangamah
Lohakam shadvidham taccha yathapurvam tadakshayam.

– *(Rasarnav-7-89-90)*[7]

This means that the sequence of the metals staying unaffected and undecayed by rusting or corrosion is gold, silver, copper, brass, lead and iron. Of these, gold rusts the least.

How to make **Copper Sulphate** from **Copper:**

Tamradaah jalairyoge jayate tutyakam shubham. When copper is mixed with sulphuric acid, we get **Copper Sulphate.**

Various ashes – When the harmful characteristics of a metal are removed by chemical action and the metal is converted to ashes, it is known as *bhasma*. The ash of iron *(lauh bhasma)*, gold (*suvarna bhasma*), silver (*rajat bhasma*), copper (*tamra bhasma*), tin (*vanga bhasma*) and lead (*sees bhasma*) are primarily used for medicinal purposes.

One chapter of Vagbhatta's *Ras Ratna Samuchchay* is dedicated to purification of juices.

Adamantine compound – In his *Brihat Samhita*, Varahmihir writes:

Ashtau seesakbhagah kansasya dvau tu reetikabhagah
Maya kathito yogoayam vigyeyo vajrasanghatah.

– *(Brihat Samhita)*[8]

This means that if a compound which has 8 parts of lead, 2 parts of bronze and one part of iron is used in the way that Maya has prescribed, it will change into a thunderbolt.

How to make distillates – According to Charak, there are nine ways of making distillates:

1. *Dhanyasava* – made from grains and seeds
2. *Phalasava* – made from fruits
3. *Moolasava* – made from roots
4. *Saraasava* – made from wood
5. *Pushpaasava* – made from flowers
6. *Patraasava* – made from leaves
7. *Kaandaasava* – made from stems and stacks
8. *Twagaasava* – made from barks
9. *Sharkaraasava* – made from sugar

Besides these, various kinds of perfumes, *itr* and other fragrant products were also developed. Detailed experiments about the metals have already been described in the metallurgy portion.

All these formulae were not given by just listening to a teacher or guru or by reading books. They were given after carrying out experiments personally. Expressing this, in the *raskalp*, a chapter of the *Rudrayaamal Tantra* of the 13th century, the scholar of chemistry says:

Iti sampadito margo drutinam patane sphutah
Sakshadanubhavairdrishto na shruto gurudarshitah
Lokanamupakarayetat sarvam niveditam
Sarvesham chaiva lohanam dravanam parikeertitam.

– *(Raskalp A-3)*[9]

"I have proved all this by carrying out the experiments myself and not by what the tutor says or what the books say and have placed the results for everyone's benefit." This is an inspiring example of the experimentation of the scholars of chemistry in the ancient times.

□

15

Botany

India has had the talent to investigate, test or examine and analyse nature since the Vedic period. Hence, in the same way, even the vegetable world was analysed. There are many references to this in ancient literature. On the basis of their appearance and other characteristics, plants were divided into seven sub-parts in the *Atharvaveda*.

1. Trees
2. Grass
3. Medicine (herbs)
4. Shrubs
5. Creeper
6. *Avataan*
7. Vegetable.

Later, in the *Mahabharata, Vishnu Puran, Matsya Puran, Shukraneeti, Brihat Samhita* and by Parashar, Charak, Sushruta, Udayan etc. vegetation, its birth, parts, acts, its types, uses, etc. were described in great detail. Some examples of which are given hereunder:

LIFE IN PLANTS

Plants are not inanimate or lifeless things; they have life. Like any animate creature, they are sensitive to cold and heat, they feel happiness and sorrow, they drink water from their roots and also fall sick, etc. We have known these facts for thousands of years. They are mentioned in many of our books.

In chapter 184 of the *Shanti Parva* in the *Mahabharata*, there is a dialogue between Sages Bharadwaj and Bhrigu. In it, Sage Bharadwaj asks that since trees can neither see nor hear, nor smell, nor feel pleasure, nor have the sense of touch, then how are they animate or living and how are they constituted by the five elements? Sage Bhrigu replied[1]:

"O Sage, although the trees seem solid, yet there is no doubt that they have the space. That is why it is possible for them to bear fruits and flowers."

"The heat that the trees have shrivels or withers the leaves, the bark, the flowers and the fruits and they fall off. Therefore, it also proves that they have the sense of touch."

"It has also been seen that when there is a loud sound like that of the harsh winds, fire, thunder, etc, the flowers and the fruits of trees fall off. This proves that trees can hear also."

"The creeper covers the tree from all sides and climbs right to the top. No one can find his way unless he can see. This proves that trees can see too."

"With pure and holy fragrance, the tree becomes healthy and grows better. This proves that they can smell also."

"They drink water from their roots and if they are suffering from some disease, we can put some medicine in their roots. This way, we can treat them too. This proves that trees have the sense of taste."

"Such as a man sucks water through a lotus stem into his mouth, likewise trees suck water through their roots upward with the help of wind."

Sukhdukhyoshcha grahanaacchinnasya cha virohanaat
Jeevam pashyami vrikshanam chaitanyam na vidyate.

"When a tree is cut, it sprouts again and they accept joys and sorrows. Hence, I see that trees also have life and that they are not non-living things."

"The wind and the heat inside the tree help it to digest the water that it takes in from its roots. Complete assimilation of the food gives it glossiness and it grows well."

Besides this, the sages Charak and Udayan have also described the feelings of life that one can observe or notice in trees and plants.

Sage Charak says: **Tachyetanaavad Chetananch**[2], meaning they (trees) also have life like living creatures. He further says **Atra Sendriyatvena Vrikshaadinaamapi Cetanatvam Bodhavyam**[3] meaning Trees also have feelings. Therefore, we must know that they too have organs and hence life.

Udayan also says,

Vrikshadayah pratiniyatbhokytradhishthitah
jeevanamaranaswapnajaagaranarogabheshaja
prayogabaajasajaateeyanubandhanuku
lopagampratikoolapagamaadibhyah prasiddha shareerawat.

— *(Udayan – prithvinirupanam)*[4]

"Like a human body, trees also experience the following feelings – life, death, dream, waking up, disease, medicinal treatment, seed, grafting, accepting what is suitable and rejecting what is not."

AN AMAZING BOOK-PARASHAR VRIKSH AYURVEDA[5]

Dr. Girija Prasanna Majumdar, the famous botanist from Bengal has, in the chapter related to Botany in his book *History of Science in India,* talked about *Vriksh Ayurveda,* a book written by Sage Parashar. N.N. Sirkar's father, who himself was a famous scholar of Ayurveda, had found the manuscript of the original *Vriksh Ayurveda.* When Majumdar read this ancient book, he was amazed because it had such a scientific analysis of the growth of a tree from a seed that it could overwhelm any reader. He translated the essence of this book into English.

This book tells the glorious story of a thousand years of India's knowledge. It was analysed at the National Symposium on Swadeshi Life Sciences in Jabalpur in 1992 by the former Human Resource Development Minister, Dr. Murli Manohar Joshi. He says that he wants to mention one more book and that is *Vriksh Ayurveda* whose writer was Sage Parashar. The scientific evaluation in it is amazing. This book is in six parts—

1. Birth of a seed
2. Vegetation
3. Shrubs
4. Vegetables
5. Creepers
6. Treatment.

There are eight chapters in the first part of the book in which the birth of a seed has been analysed in a very scientific way. The first chapter of this part is *Beejotpatti Sootradhyay,* in which Sage Parashar says:

Apohi kalalam bhutva yat pindasthanukam bhavet
Tadevam vyuhamanatvaat beejatwamaghi gacchati.

At first, the water is absorbed in the jelly like structure and a nucleus is formed and then slowly, it takes up the energy and the nutrition from the earth. Then the structure develops into an incipient seed and later, takes the form of a solid tree. This is the process of formation of protoplasm which has been described in *Beejatva Adhikaran.*

The second chapter deals with the soil. We get a detailed description of the kinds and qualities of soil.

The third chapter deals with forests. It says that there are fourteen different forests. Whenever we talk of social forestry, this will definitely be mentioned.

The fourth chapter *Vrikshang Sutradhyay* deals with physiology. About photo-synthesis, it says ***"Patraani tu vataatparanjakani abhigrihanti."***

In this, *vaat* means CO_2; *atap* means sunlight and *ranjak* means chlorophyll. This book clarifies that plants make their own food using carbon dioxide + sun + chlorophyll.

The fifth chapter *Pushpaang Sutradhyay* deals with flowers. It talks about how many kinds of flowers are there, how many parts the flowers have, what these parts are and classifies them on that basis.

The chapter on fruits *Falaang Sutradhyay* deals with the kinds of fruits, their qualities, diseases and classification. The seventh chapter *Vrikshang Sutradhyay* deals with the parts of tree. Describing these, Sage Parashar says, *patram* (leaves), *pushp* (Flowers),*moolam* (roots), *twak* (bark along with the veins), *kandam* (stem), *saram* (trunk), *sarasam* (sap), *niryasa* (excretions), *beejam* (seed), *praroham* (shoots) and their relation to each other have been described here. In the eighth chapter, the growth of a tree from a seed has been described. What has been said about the seed is very important. It is the responsibility of the present-day botanists to note how deep he went into the process of seeds and leaves. Parashar says:

Beej matrika tu beejasyam beej patrantubeejmatrikaayamadhyasthamadi Patranch matrikacchadastu tanupatrakvat matrikacchadanacchha Kanchukmityachakshate.

Beejantu prakritya dwividham bhawati ekmatrikam dwimatrikancha. Tatraikapatraprarohanam vrikshanam beejmekamatrikam bhavati. Dwi patra prarohanantu dwimatrikancha.

"Monocotyledon and dicotyledon. *Ek beej patri* and *dwi beej patri* are descriptions of the seeds, how they take the water and minerals from the earth and slowly grow into big trees. Classifying the seeds, he talks about how each seed grows."

Then he has described the functions of each part of the seed at the time of germination.

Ankurnirvrite beejmatrakaya rasah samplavate prarohangeshu. Yada prarohah swatantren bhoomyah parthivarasam grihanati tada beej matrika prashoshama padyate.

– *(Vriksh ayurveda – dwiganiyadhyaya)*

"After taking in the water and minerals and growing, until the roots are formed. At that stage, the seed leaves are not required, and they fall off."

THE TALE OF THE DEVELOPMENT[6]

The book mentions the composition of the leaves and the fruits. The food of the trees is made by the leaves. The water and minerals from the earth are brought up by carriers called *syandini*. This is the description of the 'ascent of sap'. The sap reaches the leaves where the thin veins are spread like a net. These veins are of two kinds – *upsarp* and *apsarp*.

They take the flow of the sap upwards and downwards *via* different routes. Even today's science does not have complete knowledge about how it can push the sap upwards against the earth's gravitational pull. Only with the knowledge of capillary action, can it be explained. The western countries were unaware of this for a very long time. Knowledge of the principle of capillary motion is necessary along with the knowledge of botany. What happens when the sap flows in the leaf, has been clearly explained in this book:

"Ranjaken pashchyamaanaat" means that it is digested by the process of colouring like photosynthesis. This is very important. After this, he says "***utpaadam visarjayanti***". We all know that the leaves produce oxygen in the day from photosynthesis and carbon dioxide in the night. They take carbon dioxide in the day to make their food. They throw out the excess vapour. This is known as transpiration. The book has a description of all this.

He has further said that when the excess vapour is thrown out, it creates energy. This is a description of the respiratory system. In short, it describes how the sap goes up and reaches the leaves to make food, how energy is created by transpiration. This entire process makes up a tree. Even today, no other theory, except this, about the growth of a tree, is available.

Further, while describing the structure of the **cell**, Sage Parashar says, "***Pache raskoshastu rasaspashyah aadharanch. Khalu vrikshpatre raskoshstva parisankhyeeyah santi. Te kalakeshtitena paanch bhautik guna samanvitasya rasasyashayancha. Ev ranjak yuktamanavashcha.***" This means that it is as microscopic as an atom, it has protoplasm and cell membranes. "***Kala tu sushmaccha pachaka ya bhootoshma paachita kalala dupajayate.***" This explains that this cell is created from the phase of the seed, the terrestrial juices and terrestrial energy. Sage Parashar further describes the parts of a cell. His description of the cell, which was made thousands of years ago, is a more detailed and clearer one than that made by Robert Hook with the help of the microscope in 1665. He says that the cell is composed of:

1. Outer wall
2. Gap with a colouring matter
3. Inner wall
4. Not visible to the naked eye (*Anwashch*).

Such a description of the cell is not possible without a microscope. This means that the author of *Vriksh Ayurveda,* must have had the knowledge of the microscope thousands of years ago. At that time, no one in the west knew about it. This was the scientific vision of *Vriksh Ayurveda.* If it is considered to be written even in 200 AD, then let us see as to when the west gained knowledge about the microscope and botany. It was only about 200 or 300 years ago and they have been acknowledged as great scientists and our country, which had this knowledge ages back, was called the country of snakes and snake charmers! We need to contemplate on how many years it must have taken to carry out the research and then acquire such a deep scientific foresight, because in no other country has botany been studied so long ago and in such detail as in India. However, our scholars of botany do not have this in the textbooks because they do not know Sanskrit. Whether they know the language or not, if in the future, they make Sanskrit compulsory for the science student, then the path to the history of science in this country will be wide open. How can anyone who does not know Sanskrit, learn about *Vriksh Ayurveda?*

Similarly, page 163 of the famous book *Scientific*

Heritage of India contains a classification of trees as done by Charak, Sushrit, Sage Parashar, etc. This too shows the progress of India in the field of botany.

Charak's classification[7] - In *Charak Samhita,* by Charak, vegetation has been classified in four different ways:

1. Trees - which bear fruit without bearing flowers e.g. goolar, jackfruit, etc.
2. Vegetal - Those that bear fruit after the flower e.g. mango, guava, etc.
3. Medicinal - Those fruits which fall off after ripening and becoming dry, e.g. wheat, barley, gram, etc.
4. Veerudh - which have tendrils or fibres, e.g. creepers, climbers, shrubs, etc.

Similarly, trees have also been classified according to their uses:

1. Roots - Whose roots, in comparison to other parts of the plant, are more important. They are 16 in number.
2. Fruits – Whose fruits are more useful. There are 19 varieties of plants that come under this category.

Sage Charak has divided edible plants into seven categories:

1. Bristle crop - Those that have bristles or hair on them like wheat, barley, etc.
2. Pod crop - which belong to the legume family and which have pods like beans, peas, green lentil, black gram, *arhar*, etc.
3. Leafy vegetables – Spinach, fenugreek, *bathua* etc.
4. Fruit - Different fruits.
5. Green vegetables - Various vegetables like bottle gourd, *torai* (cridged gourd), etc.

6. Food and diet—Sesame, spices, etc. which are used in food.
7. *Ikshu* (sweet juice) category—Sugar cane and its families.

Sushruta's classification[8] - Sushruta classified vegetables into ten categories:

1. Root - radish, etc.
2. Leaf - whose leaves are used.
3. Thorny leafless shrubs - whose sprouts are used, like bamboo shoots.
4. Front part - Cane, etc.
5. Fruit - All fruit bearing plants.
6. *Kaand - kooshmaand* (pumpkins), etc.
7. *Adhiroodh (*flexible) - creepers, vines, etc.
8. Skin or bark - *matulung* cinnamon, etc.
9. Flowers - *Kachnaar, etc.*
10. Fungi - Mushrooms.

Sage Parashar's classification[9] - Maharshi Parashar classified flower bearing plants into families like pod plants, *pipeelika* catkins *ganeeya, swastika ganeeya, tripundak ganeeya, mallika ganeeya and koorch ganeeya.* What is amazing is that the modern botanical classification matches Sage Parashar's classification. For example, let us see the *shamiganeeya* (leguminous) classification:

Sami tu tundamandala Vishamvidalasmrita
Panchamuktadalaishchaiva yuktajaalakarurnitaih
Dashabhih keshrairvidyat sami pushpasya lakshanam
Samee simbiphala gyeya parshva beeja bhavet sa
Vakram vikarnikam pushpam shukaakhya pushpameva cha
Etaishcha pushpabhedaistu bhidyante samijatayah.

– *(Vriksh ayurveda – pushpaangsootradhyaya)*

Shameeganeeya According to Parashar	Leguminous Modern recognition
Tundamandal	Flowers hypogamus
Visham vidal	Unequal corolla lobes
Pancha muktadal	Five true petals
Yukta jaalika	Synsephalous corolla
Dasha prikesar	Ten stamens

Similarly, there are other divisions too. Because of the expression and suitability of these Sanskrit names, Sir William Jones said, "Had Linius (the father of modern science of classification) learnt Sanskrit, he could have developed his method of giving names more perfect."

Drinking water from the roots[10] – Indians knew that plants take in liquid food, so they were called ***paadap*** (one who drinks water from the roots).

Vaktrenotpalanalena yathodharvam jalamadadet
Tatha pawanasanyuktah paadaih pibati paadapah.

"Just as if one puts the lotus stem in his mouth and sucks to drink water, similarly, with the help of the wind, the plants can drink water from their roots."

Diseases of plants[11] – Varahamihir's *Brihat Samhita* describes four kinds of diseases of plants. The modern description also has these.

Brihat Samhita	Modern
1. *Pandu Patrata*	Chlorosis of leaves
2. *Pravaal Avriddhi*	Falling of buds
3. *Shaakha Shosh*	Drying up of branches
4. *Rasa Struti*	Exudation of sap

Heredity[12] – *A Concise History of Science in India* says that Charak and Sushruta have stated that all parts of the vegetable are present in their minute forms in the fruit bearing part of the flower. These appear one by one later on.

CONTRIBUTION OF JAGDISH CHANDRA BASU

What is written above pertains to ancient times. However, even in modern times, how much does the country know about the matchless contribution of the great scientist Jagdish Chandra Basu in the field of botany?

Jagdish Chandra Basu proved that life or consciousness is not limited to humans, birds and animals alone, but in plants and other things which we consider inanimate, too.

In this manner, he presented the unanimity of life. He said that the lifeless and the living are relative words and not absolute. The only difference between the two is that metals are a little less sensitive, plants a little more, animals more than plants and humans, the most sensitive. There is only a difference of degree but there is life in each of them.

JAGDISH CHANDRA BASU'S EXPERIMENT

Around 1895, Jagdish Chandra Basu was carrying out some scientific experiment. He sent waves to a metal detector. As a result, the detector recorded some signs. When he repeated this experiment, he noticed that the picture of the sign was a little hazier each time he performed the experiment. This surprised him because this should not happen to non-living things. Being inanimate, its response must not vary, it should be the same. This is a characteristic of muscles - when they are tired, the reflexes are a little slow but they return to normal once the body has rested. This raised a doubt in his mind. He, therefore, gave the detector a little rest and then repeated the experiment. He was amazed to see the result. After a little rest, the detector started responding as earlier. He wondered why this was so? He tested it repeatedly and established the principle that even a non-living thing has sensitivity. The only difference is that it is inert.

How the western scientists reacted when Jagdish Chandra Basu expounded this theory, can be seen from the following reference. Jagdish Chandra Basu was to deliver a lecture at the Royal Scientific Society. An intellectual named Hobbes told Hartog, the famous biologist of England, "Today, Jagdish Chandra Basu, who has proved that plants and non-living things have sensitivity, is going to deliver a lecture. Will you come to listen to it?" At this Hartog's first reaction was, "I am still in my senses. I am not drunk. How did you even imagine that I will believe such a ridiculous thing?" Yet, with the idea of having fun, he attended the lecture. There were many others like him awaiting some fun. Jagdish Chandra Basu not only gave a theoretical lecture but, with the help of apparatus, he gave practical demonstrations. When he started proving his theory, all the intellectuals who had been looking on with indifference, started clapping within fifteen minutes. At the end of the session, when the Chairman asked if anyone had any doubts or would like to ask the speaker some question, no one got up. Then, Prof. Hobbes stood up and said that there was nothing worth asking and that Mr. Basu had proved his theory practically. "His lecture and the experiment would arouse curiosity but the next experiment would clarify the doubt that had arisen." Even the Chairman of the Royal Society expressed his belief in Jagdish Chandra Basu's successful attempt to prove the amalgamation of life.[13]

Later, Sir Bose made a deep study and carried out many experiments on plants and travelled around the world carrying his plants. He made many sensitive instruments which helped in looking into the minute internal changes in plants. He made the crescograph which could show the sensitivity ten million times larger. When these instruments were put on plants, it seemed as if the plants were telling us of all that they had felt during the day.

He wrote about his experiences and experiments in articles like "Unity of life, voice of life," etc. and in this modern world, proved the age old theory that plants, animals, birds, insects and in fact, the whole world has sensitivity.

□

16

Agriculture

As one enters the Udaipur Agricultural University, one sees a sign, which says,

"The line drawn by the plough is the line dividing wildness and civilisation in human history."

One finds the glorious mention of agriculture in the world's oldest book, the *Rigveda*.

Akshairma deevyah krishimit krishasva vitte ramasva bahumanyamaanah

– *(Rigveda 34-13)*

"Do not gamble, cultivate and earn with respect."

Krishirdhanya krishirmedhya jantoonaam jeevanam krishih

– *(Krishi Parashar-Shloka 8)*

"Agriculture gives you property and intellect or mental sharpness. It is the basis of human life."

Civilisation started when man started agriculture. Agriculture developed as a science in India. A short description of its history is given in *A Concise History of Science in India.*

In the Vedic Age itself, sowing of seeds and harvesting was done, instruments like the plough, sickle, sieves were developed and grains like wheat, rice and barley were grown. The honour of starting the tradition of carrying out rotational cultivation to increase the fertility of the soil, goes to the farmers of that time. According to Romesberg, the Father of Botany in Europe, the west adopted this theory much later.

In Kautilya's *Arthashastra* written during the reign of the Mauryan kings, one finds description of agriculture, agricultural production and the appointment of agricultural officials to encourage it.

Irrigation systems were also developed to help in agriculture. The Greek traveller, Megasthenes, writes that the king used to appoint officials to examine the river and the wells and also to ensure equal distribution of water to the main drains and their branches.

There are references to agriculture in the *Naradsmriti, Vishnu Dharmottar, Agni Puran* etc. *Krishi Parashar* became a reference book with respect to agriculture. It talks about the procedures in connection with agriculture.

TILLING

It talks about the area that has to be ploughed or tilled, the plough that ought to be used, its parts, etc. It also describes the kind of oxen to be used for ploughing; their colour, nature and that one must have a humanitarian outlook towards them when the work is being done.

RAIN FORECAST[1]

People of the ancient times had made an in-depth study of the changes in nature and minutely examined nature and the movements of the planets.

Describing the results due to the prominence of a certain planet at a certain time of the year, Sage Parashar says, "The year in which the sun will be the master, there will be less rainfall and human beings will have to suffer. The year when the moon is the master, there will be good rainfall and there will be a lot of vegetation. People will be healthy. Similarly, if Mercury, Jupiter and Venus are the masters of the year, the situation will remain good. However, the year that Saturn is the master, there will be distress everywhere."

TIME TO TILL THE LAND[2]

On the basis of the examination of the stars and the time, he decided when it would be ideal for tilling.

SOWING[3]

Sage Parashar expresses the opinion of Sage Garg about the best time to collect seeds when he says that the seeds must be collected in the Hindu month of *Maagh* (January-February) or *Phalgun* (February-March) and dried in the sun and then kept in a good and safe place.

MEASURING RAINFALL[4]

Krishi Parashar also has a description on how to measure rainfall.

Atha jalaadhak nirnayah:

Shatyojanavisteernah trinshadyojanamucchhritam
Adhakasya bhavenmanam munibhih parikeertitam.

– (*Krishi Parashar*)

In ancient times, the sages had developed a scale to measure rainfall. In a reservoir spread over an *adhak* that is 100 *yojan* wide and 300 *yojan* high, the quantity of rain water should be:

Yojan means the thickness of one finger

1 drona = 4 adhak = 6.4 cm

The measurement of rain today also comes to the same.

Kautilya's *Arthashastra* also talks about how to measure rainfall on the basis of drona and describes the rainfall in various parts of the country.

GRAFTING

In his *Brihat Samhita,* Varahamihir tells us two ways of grafting:

1. Cut one plant from its roots and the other plant on its trunk and insert.
2. Inserting the cutting of a tree into the stem of another. At the place where the two join, seal and cover it with mud and cow-dung.

Varahamihir also talks about which plant to graft in which season. He says:

"At the end of winter (February-March), graft those plants which do not have branches."

"During the winter season (December-January) and in Autumn (August- September) graft those plants which have a number of branches."

Speaking about how much water should be given to the grafted plants in different seasons, Varahamihir says, "Plants that have been grafted in the summer should be watered everyday, both in the morning and the evening; in winter, they should be watered every alternate day and in the rainy season, whenever the Mud becomes dry." So, we see that since ancient times, agriculture had developed as a science in India. It is because of this that the fertility of the land has remained unimpaired whereas in a few decenniums only, millions of hectares of land in America have become barren.

The praiseworthy mention of the speciality of the Indian agricultural system and its implements by the British, has been quoted in Dharampal's book, *Indian Science and Technology in the Eighteenth Century.* India was the leader in well-developed agricultural implements. Sowing in rows was considered a very good and useful method in this area. It was first used in Austria in 1662 and in England in 1730, although it started getting widely used there only fifty years later. However, according to Maj. Alexander Walker, the system of sowing in rows was prevalent in India since ancient times.[5] In a letter written to the Agricultural Board of England in 1797, Thomas Holcott said that this system had been in use in India in ancient times.[6] He sent three sets of Indian ploughs to the Board so that the British could copy them because they were more useful and much cheaper than the British ploughs.

Sir Alexander writes[7], "Probably a larger variety of seeds is sown in India than in any other country of the world. There is a tradition of harvests with nutritious roots there. I do not understand what we can give India because they already have the grains and other food products that we have; in fact, they have a much larger variety."

□

17

Zoology

According to Indian tradition, life has evolved progressively. This has been expressed in many books. The *Shrimad Bhagwad* describes:

> ***Srishtva purani vividhaanyajyaatmashaktya***
> ***Vrikshaan sarisrapapashoon khagadanshamatsyaan***
> ***Taistair atushtahridayah purusham vidhaya***
> ***Brahmavalokadhishanam mudamaapa devah.***

The basic power of the universe manifested itself in the form of creation. In this sequence, trees, reptiles, animals, birds, insects, fish, etc. were created; but this did not completely express its consciousness. Hence, human beings were created who could see that basic element.

ANCIENT INDIAN CLASSIFICATION OF LIVING BEINGS

Indian tradition speaks of about the 84 lakh species from the time that life started to the time it reached the human stage. Even modern science accepts that the amoeba passed through the one crore 44 lakh species to reach the human state. It is amazing that thousands of years ago, our ancestors realised this. Many ancient Indian scholars have classified these 84 lakh species.

All creatures were divided into two parts - *yonij* and *ayonij* (born by the combination of two or developed itself like the amoeba respectively).

Besides this, creatures have been broadly divided into three parts:

1. Aquatic - Animals that live in water.
2. Terrestrial - Animals that move on land.
3. Aerial - Animals that fly in the sky.

Again, on the basis of their birth, the 84 lakh species have been classified into four categories:

1. *Jarayuj* - Those that are born from the mother's womb like humans and some animals (mammals).
2. *Andaj* - Creatures born out of eggs.
3. *Swedaj* (Sweat born) - Small creatures which are born out of filth.
4. *Udbhij* (body-born) - Creatures born out of the earth were included in this category.

Species were classified on the basis of numbers in the *Brihat Vishnu Puran*:

1. Immovable or stationary - 20 lakhs of species
2. Aquatic - 9 lakhs of species
3. Amphibians - 9 lakhs of animals that can move on both land and water
4. Birds - 10 lakhs of species
5. Animals - 30 lakhs
6. Monkeys - 4 lakhs
7. The rest in the human species.

Each of these species was studied in detail. Animals were generally divided into two categories - Pet or domestic animals and wild animals.

Similarly, classification was also done on the basis of anatomy.[1] This is mentioned in the book *Science and Craft in Ancient India* with the help of the classifications of the various scholars. According to this, animals have been classified into—

1. One-hoofed animals like the ass, the horse, the mule, gaur, a kind of buffalo, deer etc.
2. Animals with two hooves like the cow, the goat, the buffalo, black buck, etc.
3. Animals with five fingers of their paws, like the lion, the tiger, the elephant, the bear, jackal etc. (*Science and Architecture in Ancient India*—Pgs. 107—110)

In his book entitled *Science in Sanskrit*, Dr. Vidyadhar Sharma 'Guleri' speaks about the classification of animals as given by Charak.

Charak's Classification[2] - Charak divided animals on the basis of their birth. He also classified them according to their food and habitat. (*Charak Samhita, Sootrasthan*, 27/35-54)

1. *Prasah:* Those that forcefully snatch food and eat. This class includes the cow, ass, mule, camel, horse, cheetah, lion, bear, tiger, monkey, wolf leopard, dogs with thick hair which live near the mountains, cat, rat, fox, jackals, tiger, vulture, crow, *shashaghri* (falcon-like birds that can even carry a rabbit), eagle, owl, ordinary house birds and *kurar* (the bird which pierces a fish in water and carries it away).
2. *Bhumishay*: Those who sleep under the ground. Animals that live in holes like the snake (white and black in colour) a *chitraprishtha* (one who has a

painted back), *kakuli* deer – a special kind of snake, frog, iguana, *seih* (porcupine), *gandak, kadali* (a huge cat like a tiger), mongoose, *shwawit* (*urchin*), rat etc.

3. *Animals of Anoopdesh*: Animals that live primarily in water dominant regions: the hog, a *yak* (whose tail is used to make a whisk), rhinoceros, wild buffalo, *neelgai,* deer, pig, antelope and deer with many antlers are included in this.
4. *Varishay*: Aquatic animals like tortoise, crab, fish, alligator, crocodile, oyster, otter, etc.
5. *Vaaichari*: Birds that live near water like the swan, curlew, *balaka,* heron, *karandav* (a kind of swan), *plav, asharari, keshari, maalatundaka, mrinaalkanth, madgu* (cormorant), *kaadamb, kaakatundaka, utkrosh, pundareekaaksha, chaatak jalmurga, nandimukh, sumukh, sahachari, rohini,* crane, goose, etc.
6. *Forest animals*: Animals that are born on land and live in the jungles like the cheetal (white-spotted deer), deer, *sharabh* (a deer which is huge like a camel. It has 8 legs; four on the back), *charushka* (deer family), red coloured deer, ena (black buck), sambar, *varapot, rishya, etc.*
7. *Vishkir birds*: Birds that scatter their food with their beaks and claws and then eat them. These include a quail, partridge, white partridge, red legged partridge, cock, *vartak, vartika,* peacock, *kank, girivartak, gonard, krakar* and *baarat etc.*
8. *Pratud birds*: Birds that strike and eat their food like the woodpecker, *bhringaraj* (special black coloured bird), *jeevanjeevak* (a special bird), *kokila* (cuckoo), *kairaat, gopaputra, priyaatmaj, latwa, babhru, vataha, dindimaanak, jatayu, lauhaprishtha,* weaver bird, dove, parrot, kind of deer, *chirti, sharika* (mynah), *kalawink*

(bird with a red head and a black neck), sparrow, bulbul, pigeon, etc.

Along with the above classification, Charak also gave a detailed analysis of their flesh, its uses and its effects on gout, bile and phlegm. The eggs of the partridge, hen peahen and the weaver bird, as food, have also been discussed.

Similarly, one also gets detailed descriptions of the classifications of living beings in Sushruta's *Sushruta Samhita*, Panini's *Ashtaadhyaayi*, Patanjali's *Mahabhashya*, Amarsingh's *Amarkosh*, prashastapaada's commentary on *Vaisheshik Darshan* and other books. (*Science and Architecture in Ancient India* - pp. 115–117).

TREATMENT OF ANIMALS

The *Puranas* mention, besides other things, the treatment of animals too. There is a separate portion of Ayurveda for the treatment of horses. It is called *Shalihotra*. A general introduction to horses, their styles of walking, their diseases and treatment are described in the *Puranas*. The *Agni Purana* has a detailed description on the care and treatment of horses.

The treatment of elephants and the methods to control an elephant are also given. Sage Paalakaapya's book on *Hastividya* finds a mention in the *Garuda Purana*. The *Agni Purana* also has a detailed description on the treatment of cows.

Treatment of horses in the *Shalihotrasamhita* – The Shalihotrasamhita is as significant regarding the treatment of horses as the *Charak Samhita* and the *Sushruta Samhita* are, on the treatment of human beings. It is estimated to be 800 BC. This book is also known as *Haya Ayurveda* and *Turagshastra*. The main book comprises of 12,000 *shlokas*. It is divided into eight parts. Only some parts of this book are available now. The symptoms of the disease, its treatment, medicines and how to safeguard health are given in great detail. The book has been translated into Arabic, Persian, Tibetan and English. According to veterinary specialists, this book is better than the modern books on the treatment of horses. (*Pracheen Bharat mein Vigyan Shilp* pp. 125-126)

□

18

Hygiene / Health

Once an allopath asked the famous ayurvedic physician, Pt. Shiv Sharma, what the difference between ayurveda and allopathy was. In reply, Pt. Shiv Sharma said, "When anyone comes to your clinic, you say 'a patient (sick man)' has come but it actually means a tongue, an ear, a nose, a stomach, a hand, a leg, that is a part of the body, has come; whereas, when anyone comes to an ayurveda practitioner not only does the person himself come, he also brings his food, habitat, his background with him. This means that allopathy treats only the part of the individual that is sick whereas ayurveda looks at the reason for his sickness and treats that."

This dialogue differentiates between the Indian and western outlook while deliberating on hygiene.

While speaking of hygiene here, we do not talk only about the body but also about the thoughts, feelings, climate, environment, etc.

A human being has both kinds of sorrows – the body has diseases, so does the mind. Hence, the diseases were broadly classified into two—

Aadhi (disease of the mind) and *vyaadhi* (disease of the body).

And, when we contemplate on health, it will not suffice to think on the superficial level of the body alone, but will have to be contemplated upon various other levels.

While analysing diseases in the *Yogavasishtha,* Sage Vasishtha tells Rama that diseases are of two kinds- *aadhij* and *anaadhij.*

Aadhij diseases are also of two kinds - ordinary and the essential. Ordinary diseases are those that are born out of the tensions that one incessantly suffers from one's daily behaviour and the essential ones are those that each one of us has to go through and cannot escape, like birth and death.

Anaadhij are those diseases which are not the result of any tension—like injuries, infections and toxins, which can be treated easily with the help of medicines.

When Shri Ram asked how the *aadhij* changed into *vyaadhis,* Sage Vasishtha says that a human being has many cravings and desires or passions which, if they are not fulfilled, then it saddens the mind. If that happens, then the soul or the spirit is saddened and flows uncontrolled, through our veins and nerves just as a wounded animal runs around in circles. As a result of this kind of behaviour of the spirit, the nervous system becomes disorganised leading to wrong digestion, over digestion and non-digestion, ultimately leading to defects or maladies in the body. This is known as *vyaadhi.*[1]

1. *Yog vigyan* is specially useful in order to regulate and purify our thoughts and emotions.
2. At the level of the body, ayurveda and other methods were developed for treatment. Ayurveda tries to make a person happy and healthy by studying how

the human body is made up, the initial causes for the diseases, their kinds, investigation, organising the medicine, manufacturing medicines and surgery.

India has a fairly old history of medical science. According to *Charak Samhita,* Brahma had first given Prajapati the knowledge of Ayurveda (*Sootra sthan*–1/45) and the Ashwini Kumars, who are famous as the doctors of the Gods, received it from him.

Many of their treatments have been famous, such as rejoining the head of a horse after it has been severed in a *yagya,* replanting the teeth of *Pooshan,* restoring sight to Sage Chyawan, removed his senility, etc. Indra got this knowledge from the Ashwini Kumars. Then, from him, Sage Bharadwaj, then Atreya Punarnawa, then his disciples Agnivesh, Bhel, Hareet, etc. received the knowledge. This tradition carried on further and can be divided into two parts:

1. *Dhanvantari* tradition, and
2. *Atreya* tradition.

Medicine is primary in the *atreya* tradition. Charak, whose *Charak Samhita* is very well-known, is a famous scholar of this tradition.

In the *dhanavantari* tradition, however, surgical treatment was primary. Sushruta was a famous surgeon of this tradition. His *Sushruta Samhita* is also very famous.

While deliberating on treatment, the physiology, and anatomy of the body, preparation of medicines, their kinds, uses, etc. were also given deep thought. Some of them are given below. This will make us realise how minutely we analysed this at time when the western world had not even a thought to it. We shall learn some of its main points:

1. Health – The definition of a healthy person as given

in the *Charak Samhita* is more expansive and apt than that of modern medical science.

Samadoshah samaagnishcha samadhaatumalakriyah,
Prasannatmendriyamanaah swastho ityamidheeyate.
– *(Charak Samhita)*[2]

A person whose gout, bile and phlegm, *sapta dhaatu,* purgation, etc. are all balanced and the spirit, senses and mind are in a happy state, is called a healthy person.

2. **Physiology**[3] - According to *Sushruta Shareere* 5, 6 in the *Sushruta Samhita,* the following are the main points in the construction of a body:
Skin - 7
Substrata of the elements of the human body - 7
Recipient vessels - 7
The primary fluids and contents of the body - 7
Arteries - 700
Muscles - 500
Tendons - 900
Bones - 300
Joints - 210
Vitals - 107
Veins - 24
Disorder of three humors - 3
In pure secretions - 3
Nutritional canals - 9
Sinews - 6
Woven textures - 16
Bundles of muscular bones - 16
Long rope - 4
Stitch like formations - 7
Collections of bones - 14

Parting lines – 14
Special canals – 22
Intestines – 2
Hair pores of the skin – 3½ crore

3. **Work of the heart**[4] – Western knowledge regarding the functions of the heart is very recent. The British scientist, William Harvey, had, in 1628, through his experiments, established that it was very essential for the blood to reach the heart, but he could not say how it reaches the heart. A few years later, in 1669, an Italian scientist Marshellon Malfigi revealed the process by which the blood reaches the heart. However, in the *Shatapath Brahman*, which dates back to more than seven thousand years, one finds a complete description of the entire functioning of the heart. In that, it has been said:
   Haraterdadaaterayaterhridaya Shabdah *–nirukta* –
   This means that the heart expresses the three actions of taking, giving and circulating.
   'Hr' (*harane)* means to receive; 'd' (*dane)* means to propel and 'y' (*in gatau)* means to circulate = *hridayam – shatpath brahmanam.*
   Similarly, in the *Naadi Gyanam Granth,* it is written;

   Tatsankocham cha vikaasam cha swatah kuryaatpunah punah

   The heart will itself continue the acts of contraction and expansion over and over again.
   In another book, named *Bhel Samhita,* there is a description:
   Hrido raso nissarati tasmaadeti cha sarvashah
   Siraabhirhridayam vaiti tasmaatattaprabhavaah siraah.

It is from the heart that the blood flows out and goes to the various parts of the body. It flows to the heart through the veins and the veins carry out this work in this manner.

4. **Causes of diseases**[5] – In ayurveda, the principle of the malfunctioning of the gout, biles and phlegm is the basis for the diagnosis and treatment of a disease.
   As long as these three are well-balanced, the body remains healthy. When there is an imbalance, it becomes the cause of some disease.

These three elements (*tridosha*) are present in the whole body although they appear more in some parts of the body. According to the work that they do, each of these has been divided into five parts and their effects have also been given.

Gout: This has five functions:

1. Life – Mainly respiration that is deep inspiration and expiration. (Respiratory system)
2. *Udaan* – Mainly brings out speech.
3. *Vyaan* – The carrier of the fluids of the body (Circulation of blood).
4. *Samaan* – Digestion of food, etc. (Digestive system)
5. *Apaan* – Throwing out the wastes of the body (Excretory system).

Bile: This also has five functions:

1. Digestive – Digesting the food, distributing the essence and warming the body.
2. *Ranjak* – Changing the colour of the chyle to red and converting it into blood.
3. *Saadhak* – Increases the intelligence and the brains.
4. *Aalochak* – Helps in vision.

5. *Bhraajak* – Helps in the make up of the colour.

Cough or phlegm: This also has five functions:

1. *Avalambak* – gives power and energy.
2. *Kledak* – breaks down the food grain.
3. *Bodhak* – helps in providing taste.
4. *Tarpak* – controls the eyes and the senses.
5. *Shleshak* – lubricates the joints.

It is believed that anything given to rid one of some disease, which is made from animals, vegetables or minerals, will have the five elements of juice, quality, valour, maturity and effect and each of them has been minutely analysed.

Food that is digested, dissolved and absorbed by the body, changes into the seven elements – the juices, blood, flesh, fat, bones, marrow and semen. Each of these elements is absorbed and thrown out in three ways – macro, micro and filth. It helps the body to develop slowly.

One can find a detailed description of this entire process in the *Charak Samhita* and the *Sushrut Samhita.*

Ayurvedic treatment is done in two ways—

(A) Cleansing[6] – Through five ways, which are

1. *Vaman* – getting rid of the bad things by vomiting.
2. *Virechan* – getting rid of the bad things from the anus.
3. *Vasti* – enima.
4. *Raktamokshan* – throwing out bad blood from the body caused by a poisonous bite.
5. *Nasya* – giving some greasy thing from the nose.

(B) Suppressing[7] – Treating the disease by giving medicines. This has a comprehensive sphere. Eight kinds of treatments have been given.

1. *Kaay chikitsa* – ordinary treatment

2. *Kaumaar bhrityam* - pediatrics
3. *Bhoot vidya* - psychiatry
4. *Shalaakya tantra* - treatment of the upper parts of the body like ear, nose, throat, etc.
5. *Shalya tantra* - surgery
6. *Agad tantra* - treating poison
7. *Rasaayan* - chemical treatment or chemotherapy
8. *Baajikaran* - increasing virility

MEDICINES

Charak said that nature has provided medicines in the area where a person lives. Hence, he says that one must investigate the plants and vegetables around oneself and use them. Once upon a time, many scholars of the world assembled in one place, discussions were held and the results were recorded in the *Charak Samhita*. This book talks about 341 plant-generated medicines, 177 from animals and 64 from minerals. Similarly, the *Sushruta Samhita* talks about 385 plant-generated, 57 animal-generated and 64 mineral-generated medicines and how to use them. Powders, distillates, decoctions, mixtures, gels and various other kinds of medicines were produced from these.

One finds a description of some strange medicines in books of an older period. For example, in *Valmiki Ramayana*, during the war between Ram and Ravana, when Lakshman was badly wounded and he became unconscious, Jaambawan described four rare herbal medicines for his treatment to Hanuman that are found only on the Himalayas.

Mrita sanjeevani chaiva vishalyakaranimapi
Suvarnakarani chaiva sandhaani cha mahaushadheem.

– (*Yuddha kaand* 74-33)

1. *Mritasanjeevani* – one that can give new life.

2. *Vishalyakarani* - one that can pull out the weapons that are embedded in the body.
3. *Suvarnakarani* - one that can bring back the colour of the skin.
4. *Sandhaani* - one that can heal the wounds.

After Charak, during the Buddha period, with the efforts of Nagarjuna, Vaag Bhatt and many other people, alchemy (*Rasa Shastra*) was developed. The purification and then the medicinal use of mercury was extremely result oriented. Besides this, they also developed the knowledge about converting metals like gold, silver, copper, zinc and iron into ash by soaking them in various liquids and heating them. Medicines made out of these ashes and from plants were used to cure various diseases.

SURGERY

A few years ago, a famous organisation of the surgeons of England had brought out a calendar which had the pictures of the famous surgeons of the world. The first picture was that of Sushruta. He was shown as the first surgeon of the world.

Surgery has a long history in Indian tradition.

Dhanwantari, said to be the God of Indian medicine, is also considered to be the father of surgery. The doctors of our country had made tremendous progress in this field in ancient times. Many books were written. Some writers, who need special mention, are Sushruta, Pushkalaavat, Goparakshit, Bhoj, Videh, Nimi, Kankaayan, Gargya, Gaalav, Jeevak, Parwatak, Hiranyaaksh, Kashyap, etc. Besides these writers, we also learn about the progress of Indians in this field from many other ancient books.

We find the description of diseases of the heart, stomach and the kidneys in the *Rigveda* and the *Atharvaveda*. Similarly there is a description of the nine outlets and the ten holes of the body. The surgeons during the Vedic era were brilliant in the field of brain surgery. According to the *Rigveda* (8–86–2), when Sages Vimana and Vishwak became bewildered or lost the ability to think, they were treated by brain surgery. The same book has a description of Sage Naarshad. When he became completely deaf, the Ashwini Kumars treated him and restored his hearing. The doctors at that time would easily treat a delicate organ of the body like the eye with deftness. One reads about Sage Vandan's sight being restored in the *Rigveda* (1–116–11).

Surgery developed very fast during the Buddha period. According to *Vinay Pitak,* worms started breeding in the head of a distinguished, wealthy man of the royal family. At that time, Vaidyaraaj Jeevak not only removed all the worms with surgery but smeared the wounds with a medicine. Our *Puranas* also give us a lot of information about surgery. According to the *Shiv Purana,* the Ashwini Kumars transplanted a new head when Lord Shiva severed the head of Daksh. Similarly, when Ganesh's head was cut off, an elephant's head was transplanted. We get similar examples in the *Ramayana* and the *Mahabharata.* In one place in the *Ramayana,* it has been said "***Yaajamaane swake netre udghrityaavimana dadau.***" This means that when the need arose, the eye of one man would be taken out and transplanted in another human being. (Valmiki's *Ramayana* 2–16–5). From the dialogue between Yudhishthir and Naarad in the *Sabha Parva* of the *Mahabharata,* we are introduced to the eight parts of surgical treatment.

Vaidya Sabal Singh Bhaati says[8] in the *Sushruta Samhita,* that training in surgery was given through the *guru* (teacher)-*shishya* (pupil) tradition. Practical training was given by dissecting cadavers or dummies. Trained surgeons performed surgery using various surgical instruments and through fire. If the need arose, blood transfusion was also given. For this, a sharp instrument called *shiravedh* (piercing the veins), was used.

Eight types of Surgeries – The surgeries described by *Sushruta* are:

1. *Chhedya* (to bore)

SURGICAL INSTRUMENTS AND AS DESCRIBED BY SUSHRUTA

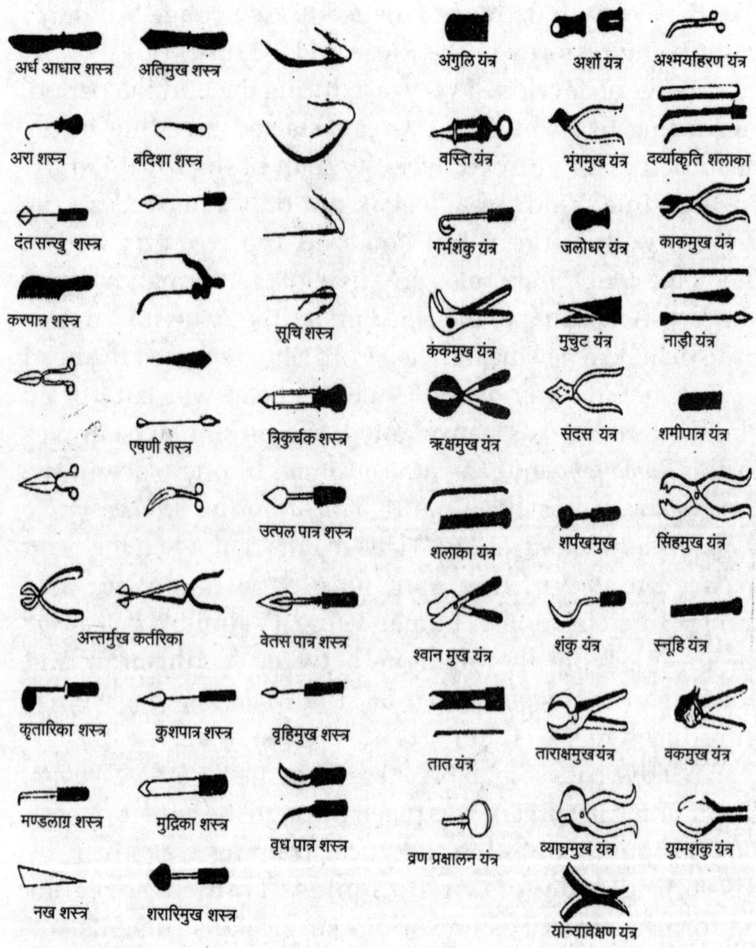

2. *Bhedya* (to pierce)
3. *Lekhya* (to separate)
4. *Vedhya* (to remove some harmful substance from the body)
5. *Aishya* (to find the wound from the veins)
6. *Ahaarya* (to remove harmful produces)
7. *Vishravya* (to remove the fluid from the body)
8. *Seevya* (to stitch the wound)

The instruments and appliances necessary to do these surgeries are also given in the *Sushruta Samhita* in detail. Some resemble the forceps and the tongs required in modern surgery. The great book written by Sushruta talks of 24 kinds of *swastiks*, 2 kinds of *sandas* (pliers), 28 kinds of needles and 20 kinds of catheters. Besides these 20, other kinds of instruments have also been described which were used for carrying out surgeries to various parts of the body. The eight surgeries that have been talked about earlier, were carried out with the help of different instruments and appliances. They were–

Ardha-aadhaar, atimukh, araa, badisha, danta shanku, eshani, kar-patra, kritarika, kutharia, kush-patra, mandalaagra, mudika, nakh shastras, sharaarimukh, soochi, trikurchakar, utpal patra, vridh-patra, vrihimukh and *vetas-patra.*

At least three thousand years ago, Sushruta had spoken about the necessity of making these instruments with the best quality steel. He even stressed that the instruments should be sharp and so pointed that even a hair could be divided into two. Sushruta has laid so much stress on the cleanliness of the atmosphere and sterilisation of the instruments used before or after the surgery, and has described the ways to do so in such a manner that even the modern surgeons are amazed. He has also talked about how to make the patient senseless (by giving anaesthesia) and the necessity to do so. In the *Bhoj Prabandh,* it is written that King Bhoj was made to smell a powder named ***sammohini*** to make him unconscious before performing surgery on his forehead.

Fourteen types of Bandages[9] - Along with these appliances, if the need arose, bamboo, crystal and some special kinds of broken rock were also used in surgery. Sushruta, who was an expert in surgery, gave a description of 14 kinds of bandages besides the six bone dislocations and 12 kinds of fractures of bones. His book also talks about 28 diseases related to the ear and 26 related to the eyes.

Sushruta Samhita also mentions surgical removal of harmful tissues born out of cancer in the intestines and also the birth of children through caesarian section. There is a mention of neuro-surgery, that is performing surgery on the nerves to rid the body of diseases and also about plastic surgery, which is the most complicated surgery of modern times. Apart from some methods which are considered as very modern ones, there is mention of some methods which are not known even to the modern medical science.

In short, it can be said that surgery was very highly developed in ancient India while the rest of the world was totally unaware of it.

Plastic Surgery in the *Sushruta Samhita*[10] - Dr. Vijay Daya (MD Anaesthesia) of Jaipur has described an experiment in plastic surgery. About 200 years ago, in 1792, there was a war between Tipu Sultan and the Marathas. In this war, four Maratha soldiers and a coach driver (Kavaasji) lost their hands and nose. A year later, a potter from Pune fixed new noses by surgery on Kavaasji and the soldiers. The potter was not just deft in making pottery with clay, he was also deft in joining parts of a human body and repairing parts by grafting the skin from some other part of the body. 'Repairing' a human body in this manner is, in modern science, called plastic surgery.

Two British doctors named Dr. Thomas Crasso and Dr. James Findlay witnessed the surgery giving Kavaasji a new nose in 1793 AD. They even drew pictures of the entire process and presented the report in the *Madras Gazette*. The same report was published in October 1794 by *Gentleman Magazine*, London. The report was as follows:—

"An artificial nose made of fine wax is placed instead of the nose that has been cut off. This wax is spread on the forehead of the person (who has to undergo plastic surgery). An outline is marked out and the layer of wax is removed. Then, the surgeon takes out the skin of the similar shape from the patient's forehead while it remains stuck to a small portion below the eyes. Because of this joint, the portion of the old nose that is left is divided into two. An incision is made behind it. Now, the skin from the forehead is brought down and stuck to the incision.

Terra Japonica (yellow *kattha)* is made into a dough after mixing it with water and spread over a piece of cloth. Five or six such pieces are placed one on top of the other and kept in the place of the surgery. After keeping this kind of a bandage for four days, a piece of cloth soaked in ghee is placed on it. After twenty days, the joined skin (from the centre of the eye) is removed and the new nose is given the proper shape. The patient has to keep lying down for the first five days after the surgery. On the tenth day, cylindrical pieces of cotton wool or soft cloth are placed inside the new nostrils to keep them open."

In the report in *Gentleman*, it has been said further, "This operation was always successful. The new nose used to stick permanently and would start looking like the old nose. Even the mark on the forehead, made by removing the skin, would vanish after sometime."

This report created ripples in the European medical

world. The surgeons from all over Europe had studied this technique thoroughly. Then, after understanding the fineness of the method, a 30-year-old surgeon, Dr. J.C. Carpew transplanted the nose of a man in 1814. This operation was also successful. This brought about a revolution in surgical treatment and it was given the name 'Plastic Surgery'. All surgeons, including Dr. Carpew unanimously agreed that plastic surgery was a gift from India.

There is no exaggeration in the above statement. Our ancestors knew the art of joining parts that had been severed and repairing broken parts of the body. A detailed description of plastic surgery is given in the *Sushruta Samhita*. Even the entire process of how the nose was transplanted on the Maratha coachman Kavaasji, is given in the *Sushruta Samhita*. The potter who had performed the plastic surgery on the coachman had probably not read Sushruta's 2500 year-old-book, but he must have inherited this art from his ancestors.

Sushruta Samhita also has a description of using the skin from the cheek to make up the nose. In today's medical science, this is known as 'facial flap'. Sushruta has, in addition, described a method of facial flap for joining an ear. Sushruta has mentioned the use of special oils, honey or ghee besides the yellow *kattha*. The surgery to join a cut lip is also the same. Actually, Sushruta, in his book, has described 300 surgical operations. These include 42 surgical processes and 121 appliances.

VACCINATION[11]

At the special session of Parliament, organised on the occassion of the golden jubilee of India's independence, Dr. Murli Manohar Joshi spoke about vaccination, one of the ancient scientific achievements of India. In his words—

"I want to place one more significant thing before you.

It is said that Dr. Jenner discovered that vaccination in 1798. However, before this, Mr. Colt had told Dr. Oliver about the vaccination that was in use in Bengal. This has been mentioned in *An Account of the Disease of Bengal; Calcutta,* dated February 10, 1731 as follows:

There are many cases of small pox in Bengal. For this, vaccination is given in the same way that Dr. Jenner had later done by making a vaccine out of the pus. In Bengal too, pus was collected from the blisters of small pox patients and stored for use the following year. The entire process has been given in detail in this journal. This is a book on medical journals and not an article from a newspaper and they have praised it wholeheartedly.

Another book entitled *Operation of Inoculation of the Small Pox as Performed in Bengal : 1731* gives these details. In reply to the question "for how long has this process been going on?" He says that this has been going on for at least 150 – 200 years and when it was asked in Bengal as to who discovered it? The villagers of Bengal and Orissa said that Dhanwantari had shown them the path. Dhanwantari is believed to be the father of Ayurveda. He is the one who came out with the pot of nectar which had been churned out of the ocean. This is that pot of nectar which Dhanwantari took to each and every village of India and protected this country from small pox and other diseases. This is the pot of nectar and it has been distributed to the gods, as the people of this land are godlike.

CLONING IN THE *MAHABHARATA*[12]

Will you believe that now one can make a uterus or a kidney inside one's body itself? Even 25 years ago, no one would believe what Dr. Matapurkar had said. But, he proved that just as a tree brings out a fresh branch where one has already been cut off or just as the lizard grows a new tail after dropping its old one, the same is also possible with a human body. On the basis of a stem cell, the uterus, kidney, in fact, even the intestines can be made. On one hand, while American scientists claim to have made a human clone in the laboratory, Dr. Balakrishna Ganapat Matapurkar has already received the patent for reproducing any part of the body by taking out the stem cells from that part.

He wrote the first article on this technique in 1991, but, in that, he did not say how this was possible. The reason was that the world community, at that time, was not ready to digest the fact of developing new organs from the stem cell. This article was the result of fifteen years of very hard work. In 1999, he revealed that the basis of what he had written about the creation of a part inside the body was the stem cell. Cloning depends completely on the principle of stem cell.

Human embryo is made up of only three cells. It is from these cells only that the whole body is developed later on. Stem cell is one of these, and is found in every part of the body. Matapurkar used this cell to make up the new parts and tissues. The experiments done on monkeys and dogs were successful and through this process itself, he developed a uterus within three months. Now experiments on human beings have started. Negating the apprehensions about the biological disorder completely, he says, "A human body itself is such a factory which supplies the raw material to manufacture a new part. Hence, the question of disorder does not arise. Lakhs of people die every year because of kidney failure. This technique will change the entire scenario."

You will probably be even more amazed to read that Matapurkar does not consider his research new. He says, "There is nothing new in what I have done. Our ancestors had done this in the age of the *Mahabharata* itself. One day, a question suddenly arose in my mind that if we consider the *Mahabharata* to be true, then how would Gandhaari have given birth to 100 children? I found the answer to this question in Chapter 115 of the *Adi Parv* in the *Mahabharata*. I was surprised to read that it had the description of the entire scientific process of giving birth to 100 Kauravas from the stem cell. I realised on that day that I was not doing anything new."

The descrition in the *Adi Parv* of the *Mahabharata* is as under:

Kunti had given birth to a son who had the brilliance of the sun. When Gandhari, who despite having conceived for two years had not had a child, heard this, she was disturbed and aborted herself. A blob of flesh as hard as iron, came out. Sage Dwaipaayan Vyas was called in. He examined that blob of flesh. He cooled it in a pot and secured it by wetting it completely with special medicines. Then, he divided this into 100 parts and put each part securely in separate vessels full of ghee for two years. After two years, the 100 Kauravas were born serially.

While studying, his imagination started working. He says that his interest in gardening is the source of this imagination. When he sees a plant sprouting out of a cell and later, when he sees new branches coming out after pruning, he realises that 'nature has a treasure of intelligence'. Born in Gwalior in 1941, Matapurkar received his degree in surgery from Gajra Raje Medical College. Then, while working in the Maulana Azad Medical College, he developed the technique of making the parts of the body rather than transplanting them. He regrets the fact that the majority of Indian doctors only follow the west and consider them to be the best. He says, "There is nothing more ironical than the fact that people acknowledged my work only after it got a patent in America. Is this not mental slavery?" Seeing his work, three institutions have been started in the US and multinational companies are spending billions of dollars on this project. When he applied for the American patent in 1996, the US had started, for the first time, to work on the 'stem cell'. In fact it was only after his research that the word stem cell came into vogue.

Human cloning is an effort to create an identical human being but Matapurkar's technique is to remake the parts of the body. Creating an identical person is not just against nature, it is also immoral. Matapurkar says that the technique should be such that it should make human life better. Matapurkar does not want to use his technique commercially. He wants the students to learn this technique so that it soon becomes a general process of treatment. In his words, research is the name given to a craze or a mania which requires imagination, submission, patience, hard work and the strength to struggle. He has his own definition of a meaningful life. He seeks the help of a Marathi *shloka* of Swami Ramdas and says *"marave pari keerti roope urave"* meaning that everyone has to die but one's fame must live on and Matapurkar has shown this. The last line of the patent he has received is—"this discovery can really create parts of a human body and can make them new."

CHILD WITH SPECIAL QUALITIES

The American Genetic Association brings out a journal *The Journal of Heredity*. In its 75:152 - 154-1984 edition, there was an article by Alain F. Corcos of the Michigan State University entitled 'Reproduction and Heredity Beliefs of the Hindus Based on Their Sacred Books.'

This has the description of the procreation section of the ***Manusmriti, Brihatsamhita*** of Varaahamihir and specially the *Brihadaaranyak Upanishad*. According to these it has been said that one must eat a special kind of food for a special kind of child.

The *Brihadaaranyak Upanishad* says:

1. To get a fair complexioned child with a long life, one who has knowledge of one *Veda,* one must have milk and rice with ghee along with his wife.
2. To get a golden coloured child with a long life, who has knowledge of two *Vedas,* one must eat rice and curd with ghee along with his wife.
3. To get a dark complexioned child with a long life, and knowledge of three *Vedas,* one must eat water with rice and ghee along with his wife.
4. Those who want a daughter who has a long life and is brilliant, must feed one's wife *khichadi* made of rice and sesame seeds.
5. Those who desire that their son should have knowledge of the four *Vedas,* be a famous scholar must eat *khichadi* made of rice and *urad daal* with ghee and a medicine named *Rishabh,* along with his wife.

After giving a description of these and other books, the author asks if there is any truth in all these. Then, answering in the affirmative, he writes that this have been proved right by studies conducted by French and Canadian physicians. According to them, magnesium, potassium, calcium and sodium play a role in determining the sex of the child. Excess of potassium and sodium and less of calcium and magnesium is the cause of the birth of a son and vice versa. Stalwoski conducted this experiment on 36 couples and gained success in 31 that is 83 per cent while Lorain conducted the tests on 224 couples and gained success in 181, that is 81 per cent cases. Why this happens, he does not know - probably, a special diet influences the process of uniting the *X* and *Y* chromosomes.

This study tells us that instead of ignoring the ancient references, we must acknowledge that there could be great truths in them - truths which we do not know, probably whose knowledge will help us serve humanity better.

□

19

Science of Sound and Voice

The process of the creation of the universe started with sound. The initial sound started with the Big Bang. The root sound, (primordial resonance) symbolised by the 'OM', is known as *Naadabrahma.* In the *Paatanjal Yogasootra,* the sage Patanjali has described it as ***'tasya vaachak pranavah'***. In the *Maandukyopanishad,* it has been said –

> ***Omityetadaksharamidam sarvam tasyopavyakhyanam***
> ***Bhootam bhavadbhavishyaditi sarvamonkara eva.***
> ***Yachyaanyat trikaalaateetam tadapyonkara eva,***
>
> – *(Maandukyopanishad–1)*

This means that '*OM*' is the indestructible form. This entire world is nothing but another interpretation of it. Whatever has happened, whatever is there and whatever is going to happen is all the world of '*Omkar*'. In fact, any other element which is older than the three periods of time, is also *Omkar*.

This *Aadi Naad* is expressed in various forms in the

universe. In human beings, it is expressed as their voice.

FORMS OF SOUND

The science of sound has been studied in great depth in our country. There is a *richa* in the *Rigveda:*

> ***Chatwaari Vaak Parimita Padaani Taani Vidurbrahmana ye manishinah***
> ***Guha treeni nihita nengayanti tureeyam vaacho manushya vadanti.***
>
> – *(Rigveda 1-164-45)*

Sound has four forms which the wise men knew of. Of these, three are latent in the body but the fourth can be experienced. Giving a detailed explanation of this, Panini says the four forms of sound are:

1. *Para*– that is transcendental.
2. *Pashyanti*– that is pictorial.
3. *Madhyama*– that is intermediary.
4. *Vaikhari*– that is articulate speech.

ORIGIN OR BIRTH OF SOUND

The origin of sound was experienced in great depth. On this basis, Panini says, "*Atma,* the soul, is that basic foundation where the sound originates. That is its first form. It is a subject of experience. It cannot be heard with the help of any instrument. This form of sound is *para.*

Later, when, with the help of the intellect and meaning, the spirit sees a picture of an object or an action, it is called *pashyanti* or pictorial. A picture of whatever we say, is first formed in our minds. So, the second phase is *pashyanti.*

Next, after inspiring the energies of the mind and the body, starts a muttering which cannot be heard. This muttering rises and with the help of the breath, comes to the throat. This form of sound has been called *madhyama*.

All these three forms cannot be heard. Then, rising further, the muttering, with the help of the touch parts above the throat, comes out in various forms of sound as the *sarvaswar, vyanjan, yugmaakshar* and *matra*. This sound, that can be heard, is called *vaikhari*. All knowledge, science, behaviour and expression of communication is possible only through this.

EXPRESSION OF SOUND

We see here, how minutely our sages had studied the sound that emits from the mouth and also which part helps each letter to come out. Their analysis is so scientific that you cannot bring out that sound from any other part or in any other way.

Ka, kha, ga, gha, nva – These have been called *kanthavya* because they come out from the throat (*kanth*) when you try to pronounce them.

Cha, ccha, ja, jha, iyan – These have been called *taalavya* because while pronouncing them, the tongue touches the palate (*taalu*).

Ta, tha, da, dha, na (ट, ठ, ड, ढ, ण) – These have been called *moordhanya* because pronouncing them is possible only when the tongue touches the upper part of the hard palate (*moordha*).

Ta, tha, da, dha, na (त, थ, द, ध, न) – These have been called *dantavya* because the tongue touches the teeth (*dant*).

Pa, pha, ba, bha, ma – These have been called *oshthya* because they can be pronounced only when the lips (*oshth*) meet.

SCIENCE OF THE VOWELS

The pronunciation of all alphabets, compound words, etc. is based on vowels. Hence, that was also studied and experienced in great depth. As a result of this, it was established that vowels are of three kinds:

1. *udatta* - loud voice
2. *anudatta* - ignoble or low voice
3. *swarit* -medium voice.

They were analysed even more minutely. This became the basis of music. Seven notes were accepted in music, which are known by the symbolic signs of *sa, re, ga, ma, pa, dha, ni* (do, ray, ma, fa, so, la, ti) These seven notes were divided into three basic notes.

Ucchairnishaad, gandharau neechai rrishabhdhaivato
Sheshastu swarita gyeyah, shadaj madhyampanchamaah.

Nishaad and gaandhaar (ni, ga) are loud; *rishabh and dhaivat* (re, dha) are low and *shadj, madhyam* and *pancham* (sa, ma, pa) are medium.

With the different combinations of these seven notes, different ragas were created. The various sound waves created by the singing of the different ragas have an affect on humans, animals and nature. Even this has been very minutely analysed here.

With the specialised chanting of some particular mantras, certain vibrations are created in the atmosphere. These have special effects. This is the basis of the science of spell, chanting or the *mantras*. Its sensibility can be experienced by listening to the chanting of the mantras or meditating under the dome of a temple.

From ancient times, there are many references to the singing of the various ragas and their impacts. There are different ragas for different moods - for the evening, or morning; for joy, sorrow, excitement, pity. Earthen lamps would light up with the singing of raga *Deepak* and it would start raining when raga *Megh-Malhaar* was sung. We find similar examples in modern times too.

Some experiences–

1. The famous vocalist, Pandit Omkar Nath Thakur, went to Florence, Italy in 1933 to participate in the All World Music Conference. At that time, Mussolini was ruling. Panditji told Mussolini about the significance of the Indian ragas. He replied, "I have not been able to sleep for the past few days. Tell me if your music has some speciality." At this, Pt. Omkar Nath Thakur picked up his *taanpura* and started singing *raag Pooriya (Komal Dhaivat)*. In a short while, Mussolini fell into deep sleep. Later on, he praised Indian music wholeheartedly and ordered the head of the Royal Academy of Music to record Panditji's voice and song.[1]

   Today, with the western influence on the values of our lives and our behaviour, the younger generation is getting attracted to Western pop music. What are the results of music? Western pop music becomes the cause of frustrating our inner personalities and increases our inferiority complexes; whereas, Indian music is a medium of developing sublime feelings and bringing equilibrium to our lives.The following experiments will make it clear.

2. Shri Ma conducted an experiment in the Auriobindo Ashram, Pondicherry. In two different places on a piece of land, same particular seeds were sown. Pop music was played near one of them and Indian music near the other. With the passage of time, the seeds sprouted and the plants started growing. What was amazing was that the plant before which pop music was played grew to be unbalanced and its leaves

were undeveloped and broken. However, the plant before which Indian music was played, was balanced and its leaves were well-developed and well-formed. Seeing this, Shri Ma said, "Both musics have a similar effect on the inner personality of a human being as they had on the plants."

3. When we listen to music, we must notice one thing very minutely. This will help us understand the nature and result of western pop as well as Indian music. When Pt. Bhimsen Joshi or Pt. Jasraj or any other artist sings at a concert, the audience nod their heads in appreciation. On the other hand, when western pop music is played and when one hears the screaming and shouting of a Michael Jackson or a Madonna, the legs of the audience start shaking. Thus, it can be realised that while Indian music develops the feelings of a human being above the navel, western pop music increases the feelings below the navel, which destroys the inner personality of a human being.

SOUND VIBRATIONS[2]

When we strike a bell, its sound can be heard at a distance. How does this happen? Explaining the process, Vatsyayan and Udyotkar say that a certain kind of vibration takes place when the bell is struck. Some atoms move because of the blow and combined with *sanskaar,* which is known as *kamp santaan sanskaar,* create a vibration and with the help of the air, are carried forward. These are heard in an uninterrupted manner. Vibration causes this.

ECHO[3]

Vigyan Bhikshu, in his *Pravachan Bhaashya,* chapter 1 *sootra* 7, asks what is echo? Explaining this, it has been said that just as one's image, which can be seen in the mirror or in water, is called reflection, similarly, when sound strikes against something, it rebounds, and is called an echo. Just as the reflection in the mirror or in water is not the true image, similarly an echo is not the true sound either.

Roopavattvam cha na saamaanya tah pratibimba prayojakam shabdaasyaapi
Prati dhwani roop pratibimba darshanaat

– *(Vidvaan Bhikshu, pravachan bhaashya,a1 sootra 87)*

PITCH INTENSITY AND TIMBRE[4]

According to Vaachaspati Mishra ***'Shabdasya asaadhaaran dharmah'*** – there are the many characteristics of sound. In *Tatva Chintaamani*, Gangesh Upadhyayji says, **"vaayoreva mandatar tamaadikramena mandaadi shabdotpattih".** Gentle and loud sounds are created with the assistance of wind.

Scholars like Vaachaspati, Jaimini, Udayan, etc. have, in their books, analysed the generation of sound, its vibrations, echoes, its intensity, softness and its results thousands of years ago. All this is amazing even today.

□

20

Science of Writing (Script) or Graphemics

Many western scholars in the 18th and 19th centuries, tried to spread the illusion that the ancient sages were ignorant in the art of writing and that the root of the Brahmi and other scripts that developed in India in 300-400 BC, was outside India. In this context, Dr. Orfreed and Mueller ascertained that the Indians learned writing from the Greeks. Sir William Jones said that the Indian Brahmi script developed from the Semetic script. Prof. Banfre and Prof. Baver tried to prove the fact that the Phoenician script was the foundation of the Brahmi script. Dr. David Deringer felt that Brahmi was born out of the Aramaic script. While writing the history of Sanskrit literature, in the context of script, Max Mueller established his opinion that the art of writing was known to in India since 400 BC only.

Unfortunately, later on, Indian scholars also started singing the tune of the west and supported their conclusions. In this process, they did not make much effort to learn about the script and its development as given in the books and the country's tradition.

In this situation, let us see what the reality is.

Famous archeologist and specialist in scripts, A.B. Walawalkar and scribe L.S. Wakankar have, through their research proved that the Indian script originated in India itself and said that on the basis of phonetics, the tradition of writing was present even in the Vedic times. This is proved by many archeological evidences too.

In his article on typography, Eric Gill describes the hurdles in ideal phonetic writing by saying that at sometime, some sound must have been synonymous with some sound but with the study of the Roman script, one does not remember that a letter would always have the same sound. For example, 'ough', these four letters together are pronounced in seven different ways – 'ode', 'uff', 'of', 'aau', 'o', 'uu', 'ao'. In his conclusion, Gill writes that in his opinion it would be foolish to say that the Romans letters write and print the sound very well.[1]

On the other hand, India has had a long history of phonetic writing. Some examples of this are available in our ancient books:

1. There is a story in the *Yaju Taittareeya Samhita* that once the gods faced the problem that since sound vanishes once the words are spoken out (i.e. sound it is shapeless), what method could be applied to give it a shape? So, they went to Indra and said, "Vaachanvya kurveet" which meant, grant sound a shape. Then Indra said that he would have to take the help of the *Vaayu,* (wind). The gods agreed and Indra gave a shape to sound in the form of the knowledge of writing or script. This is famous as *Indra vayavya vyaakaran* that is, the grammar pertaining to the aerial Indra. This is more popular in the South.
2. The following lines from the *Ganak Rishikrit Sookta*

Ganapati Atharvasheersha give clear proof of the birth of writing.

Ganadim poorvamucchaarya varnaadim tadanantaram. Anuswaarah paratarah. Ardhendulsitam. Taarena ruddram. Etattavamanuswaroopam. Gakaarah poorvaroopam. Akaaro madhyaroopam anuswaarashrachaantyaroopam. Binduruttar roopam. Naadah sandhaanam. Samhita sandhih. Saisha ganesh vidya.

This means first pronouncing the group of sounds, then writing them in the proper sequence with the help of colour and then, putting a dot (which marks the nasal sound). This way, O Ganesh! Your picture will be thus – ga will be a consonant and the part in the middle will be the *akaar roopadand* and the last will be a vowel. The sound and the correct pronunciation is *Ganapati vidya,* that which only Ganesh knows.

3. Shiva was the deity who gave the source of sound. Because of the death of people the branches of the various *Vedas* started disappearing. Hence, with a prayer to save them, the Sanak and other saints went to Shiva in Chidambaram in the South. Hearing their prayers, Lord Shiva played his *damru* nine and five, i.e. fourteen times during the interval of his cosmic dance. With this, fourteen sources of sound were born. These came to be known as the *Maaheshwar sootra*. Describing them, it has been said:

Nrittavasaane nataraajaraajo nanaad dhakkam navapanchavaaram
Uddhartukaamah sanakaadisiddhaan etadwimarshe Shivasootrajaalam.

– *(Kaushik Sootra –1)*

Panini talks about the 14 *Maaheshwar sootras* as follows:

1. a, i, u, na
2. ri, lri, k
3. e, o, unva
4. ai, o ch
5. ha, ya, va, ra, t
6. la, nha
7. inya, ma, angh, unva, nha, na, m
8. jha, bha, inya
9. dha, tha, gha, sh
10. ja, ba, ga, da, d, sh
11. kha, pha, cha, tha, tha, cha, ta, tra, ya
12. ka, pa, y
13. sh, sh, sa, ra
14. ha, l

Iti Maaheshwaraani sootraani

4. The sages developed many complex methods like *jata, maala, shikha, rekha, dand, rath, dhwaj and ghan* for remembering and ensuring the purity of the *Vedas*. All this was difficult to retain without writing.
5. When Ved Vyas was thinking of writing the *Mahabharata,* he faced the problem of who should write it. To solve this problem, he thought of Ganeshji - ***kaavyasya lekhanaarthaya ganesham smartyatam mune'*** and when Ganeshji came, Sage Vyas said to him, ***'lekhako bharatasyaasya bhava gananaayakah'*** that is "You be the writer of the Bharat granth". This means that Ganesh was a renowned scribe of that time.

Panini has critically discussed in his study of the *Rigveda* that when the voice comes to its fourth state, that is *Vaikhari*, then, with the help of the five parts of the body, sound is born. On this basis, the parts of the body that the vowels and the consonants are related to are classified as under:

1. *Kanthya* – Breath comes out from the throat. The sound that comes out then includes the alphabets 'a', 'aa', 'ka', 'kha', 'ga', 'gha', 'na', 'ha' and *visarga* that is the colon like sign.
2. *Taalavya* – When the breath comes out at the palate near the teeth above the throat, the sound is expressed through the sounds of 'I', 'ee', 'cha', 'ccha', 'ja', 'jha', 'ian', 'ya' and 'sh'.
3. *Moordhanya* – take the tongue a little backward, touch it to the soft palate and bring out the sound. This is expressed in the alphabets 'ri', 'rri', 'ta', 'tha', 'da', 'dha', 'na' and 'sha'.
4. *Dantya* –The tongue touches the teeth. The sound that comes out then, brings out the alphabets 'iri', 'la', 'ta', 'tha', 'da', 'dha', 'na', 'lə' and 'sa'.
5. *Oshthya* – The alphabets that are pronounced by joining the two lips are 'u', 'oo', 'pa', 'pha', 'ba', 'bha', 'ma' and 'va'.

Besides this, 'ai', 'aee', 'o', 'au', 'an', 'ahh' are mixed vowels.

On the basis of the above science of sound, the script developed. With the flow of time, the scripts kept changing, but their basis was the fundamental principle of the science of sound. Famous archaeologist Balaawalkarji studied the scripts of the ancient coins and proved that it was mainly the *Maaheshwari* script which was the vedic script. Later, the Brahmi and the Nagari script developed from this. We

THE STRUCTURAL ELEMENTS OF DEVANAGARI SCRIPT

(BASED ON PRINCIPLES DEDUCED BY A. B. WALAWALKAR IN 'PRE-ASHOKAN BRAHMI')

WALAWALKAR'S CONSTRUCTION OF VEDIC MAHESHWAR CRESCENTS

VEDIC 'OM'

A-U-M PURANIC 'OM'

L. S. WAKANKAR'S CONSTRUCTION

K CLASS · CH CLASS · TA CLASS · T CLASS · P CLASS

पाणिनी

अ कु ह विसर्जनीयानां

इ चु य शानां

ऋ टु र षा णां

लृ तु ल सा नां

उ पु - उपध्मानीयानां

	VOWELS	HARD	HARD-ASP.	SOFT	SOFT ASP.	NASALS	Semi Vowels	Sibilants	CONJUNCTS
कंठः GUTTARALS	अ A	क Ka	ख Kha	ग Ga	घ Gha	ङ N	ह Ha	An	क्ष Ksha
तालु PALATALS	इ I	च Cha	छ Chha	ज Ja	झ Jha	ञ N	य Ya	श Sha	ज्ञ Jna
मूर्धा LINGUALS	ऋ R	ट T	ठ Tha	ड Da	ढ Dha	ण N	र Ra	ष S	श्र Shra
दंताः DENTALS	लृ L	त T	थ Tha	द Da	ध Dha	न Na	ल La	स Sa	त्र Tra
ओष्ठौ LABIALS	उ U	प Pa	फ Pha	ब Ba	भ Bha	म Ma	व Va		
	O	I	II	III	IV	V	VI	VII	

Chart Made By : L. S. WAKANKAR, 1967

can see this in the table made by famous archeologist L.S. Wakankar.

ARCHAEOLOGICAL EVIDENCES[2]

While referring to the research and proof by Walawalkar and Wakankar, based on the development and archeological proofs of script, the thoughts that Dr. Murli Manohar Joshi has expressed in his article *Lipi Vidhaataa Ganesh*, prove that the art of writing was an entity in India and that it was based totally on the science of sound. This is not seen in the other scripts of the world. In Dr. Joshi's words:

"Let us now discuss some of the proofs received from archeology.

There is a seal in the British Museum (31-11-366/1067-47367-1881), whose imitation is exhibited in picture 1. In this 6th century BC seal, Babylon's wedged letters and the Brahmi scripts appear side by side. The wedged script had been read in 1936 itself, but the middle line was left because it was thought to be an unknown script. Epigraphist Walawalkar read this unknown script and disproved the European scholars' belief that India had borrowed the script from outside. According to him, this seal presents the proof that it is before Ashok's time, and its language and script are Sanskrit and Maheshwari respectively. The line reads *'avakhegyaraagkh nu auharmanubhyah dadatu'* which is the Sanskrit confirmation of the article that was wedged scripted on it. This proves Mc Donald's and Beuhlar's theory wrong that India had borrowed the script from outside five centuries before Christ. Similarly, there is another important proof in the Louvre Museum in Paris. It is a 3000-2400 BC seal procured from the King of Sargon in the excavations carried out in Palestine. Seeing the seal (picture 2), John Marshall had said that the archaeological findings of this seal are startling. Its similarity with the Indus Valley seal (picture 3) has put question marks on the European scholars' theory that the Indian script had been borrowed from outside. Now, the hue and cry that our ancient scholars had borrowed the script from outside has quietened down.

Picture-1

But the scholars with a British mindset are silent over the ancientness of the Indian script."

Picture-2

Picture-3

Picture-5

Picture-4

Picture-6

Picture-7

VEIDIC OMKAR

In this sequence, it is also necessary to take a glance at the 6th century BC, Sohagara copper transcript. The first line of the transcript has the same picture which has been called Veidic Omkar in the list drawn by Walawalkar. Look at pictures 5, 6 and 7. These are pictures of coins which have spiritual symbols like the Veidic Omkar and the Swastik embossed on it. The question is, why should we agree that the Veidic Omkar was like this? Describing the creation of the Omkar, it is written in the *Gyaneshwari:*

> ***a-kaar*** **charanyugal** ***u-kaar Udar vishal***
> ***m-kaar mahaamandal; mastakaakaare. 19***
> ***he tinhi ekavatale. techa shabdabrahma kavakala***
> ***tey miyan gurukripa namile, adi beej. 20***

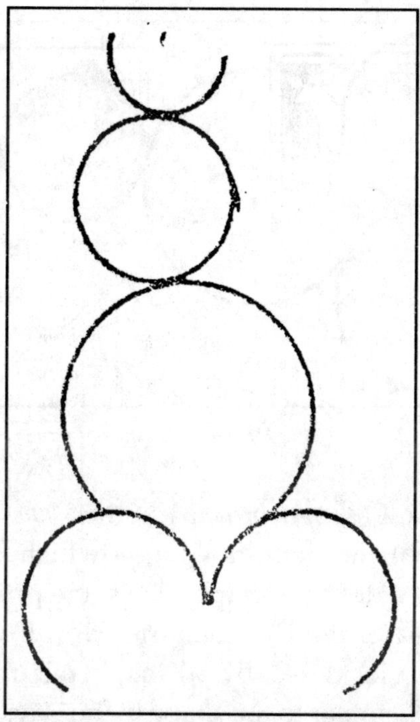

Picture-8

The description of the *Shabd brahma* or *ekakshar brahma,* or the form of *Pranav* in the *Gyaneshwari* is very important. OM as it is written in the present Devanagari script does not show a similarity to this description, though it is very similar to the Veidic Omkar of Walawalkar. If we look at the Ardhenndu principle of the *Maheshwari sootras,* we can solve this mystery. Look at **picture 8.** The two semi-circles at the bottom represent the **'a',** there is another semi-circle above that. This represents the **'u'** and above that is a full circle and a semi-circle, which exhibits the **'m'.** Thus, the *Omkar* of *Gyaneshwari*, the *Ekakshar Brahma* of the *Gita* and the *Upanishads* or the *Pranav*, are all in definite shapes or

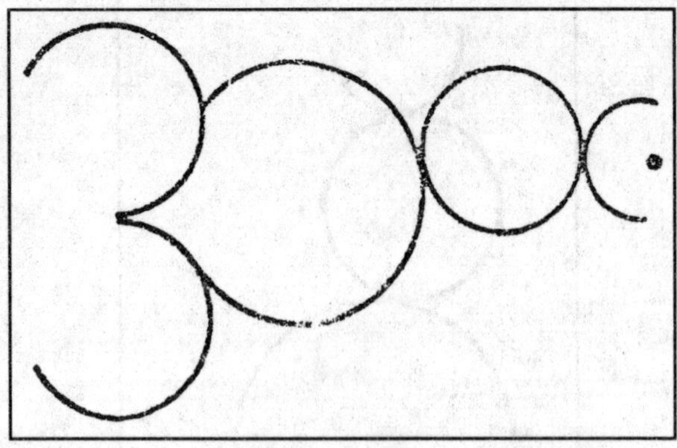

Picture-9

forms as per the *Ardhendu principle* of the *Maheshwari Sootras*. These represent the definite sounds which, when joined serially, forms a definite shape. The same principle can be seen in the OM of the Devanagari script. If we move the Veidic Omkar clockwise, by 90° as in picture—9, then it looks strikingly similar to the shape in the Devanagari script. In a way, the journey of the change of the Vedic Omkar to the Devanagari OM, is the story of the development of the Indian script. It can be seen from the *Rigveda* to the *Padm Puraan*.

□

21

Theoretical Science – Western and Indian Thinking

Pure science is another form of science. This includes the study and contemplation of some basic questions. What is the universe? What is the ultimate truth about it? What are the powers that direct the universe? What are its rules? What is the characteristic of each unit of the universe and their mutual relations?

Countries of the west and India - all contemplated and analysed these questions and came to some conclusions, but their paths were different. As Swami Vivekanand said, western science, through extensive analysis and experiments of the outer world, moved towards finding answers to these questions, whereas India moved forward by seeing a little of the outside world but more of the inner self. Both drew conclusions from their explorations and on their basis they formed a philosophy and an outlook which influenced the various mutual relations of the entire world.

In the next few pages, we shall analyse briefly, the explorations carried out by the west and by India, and their consequences.

SCIENCE-JOURNEY OF WEST

(A) According to the ancient Greek philosophers, the world is made up of four elements - earth, water, air and fire. Some philosophers believed that the world was molecular. They all had a biological outlook towards the world. This philosophy was influential in the west till 1500 AD but in the 16th and 17th century, the west saw many basic changes in the field of science. These changes really shook the basic ideology that the west had till then. The main people behind these changes were Francis Bacon, Rene Descartes, Galileo and Newton.

(B) In order to gain knowledge of the world, Francis Bacon set forth a mathematical process according to which one should first experiment, then draw general conclusions and then again test it by experimenting. Whatever one finds correct, would be correct and the rest would all be wrong.

Not accepting the traditional methods of study, Rene Descartes said that all knowledge which speaks of possibility is worth rejecting and all knowledge that is decisive and beyond doubt is acceptable. He has described this method in his book *Discourse on Method.* In this book, he has established that if one wants to resolve a problem, one must break it up into small portions and then assemble them logically. This analytical process became a big gift to modern science.

Galileo tried to investigate by using instruments and on the basis of the examination of the planets, challenged the concept of a world with the earth at the centre and established that the earth went around the sun and not vice versa.

Just as Descartes spoke about breaking the world

into small pieces and then understanding it, Galileo opened the door to examine space. Later, the west's scientific journey moved forward to discover the minutest particle of the universe and to measure the expanse of the universe.

Initially, in the search of the smallest part of the universe, it was believed that this world is a collection of elements, compounds and mixtures. As the search progressed, they said that the element was the basic matter and that it was indivisible. Around 92 kinds of elements were discovered and it was believed that the entire world was a collection of these. However, Avogadro and Dalton proved that an element is not the basic particle, but are made up of very tiny particles and named them molecules and atoms.

Newton combined all these scientific facts and presented the picture of a complete universe. With his intelligence, he developed a new mathematical theory called **differential calculus** and included Kepler's theory of **planetary motions** and Galileo's **Law of falling bodies** to his own laws of motion, through which one could interpret or explain and control the motion of an ordinary stone and the massive planets and stars. Based on this, Newton presented his own model of the universe.

According to Newton, only time and space are endless. Among them, space is uniform while time is simple linear. Out of this time and space, from small particles of dust and sand, the massive planets and stars are made. They have been made up by these small particles and these particles get their motion from gravitational power. With his laws of motion, Newton explained the laws of the motion of the planets and established that the entire universe follows these laws.

Newton's theory of the universe as machine was dominant over the entire western world for about three hundred years.

(C) By the end of the 19th century and the beginning of the 20th century, two big theoretical systems in the field of science, came into existence. These gave a big jolt to Newton's theory of a mechanical universe and that the world is made up of small particles of atoms.

These were the 'Quantum Theory', which was related to the basic unit of power and the Theory of Relativity which was related to space, time and the structure of the entire universe.

Maxwell, Max Planck, Madame Curie, Rutherford, Neils Bohr, Werner Heisenberg, James Chadwick, Lui De Broglee, Irwin Schrodinger, etc. also contributed in the establishment of the Quantum Theory.

1. Until the middle of the 18th century, an atom was considered indivisible. However, German physicist Helmholtz believed that electricity has positive and negative charges and just as the elements are made up of atoms, electricity too is made up of partilces. Later, Thomson, Hertz, etc. proved through experiments that electricity is made up of small particles called **electrons.** They keep moving around the nucleus of the atom. Rutherford and Neils Bohr established the planetary form of the atom.

   Later, the nucleus of the atom was broken and the positively charged **proton** and the charge-free **neutron** were discovered. Einstein proved that light is nothing but a flow of photons, which is different from electromagnetic particles. During the process of this discovery, till 1963, about 200 particles like meson, pion, nion, hyperon and neutrion, etc. were also discovered and it seemed as though a jungle of particles had come up.

Many particles were discovered but when science tried to find out the truth about these, a problem arose – the solution to which has still not been found. If we want to find the composition of an electron, then we will have to find out about the speed and direction of the electron. To find out the direction, we will have to use gamma rays. But an electron, which changes its form when it strikes against an ordinary photon of light, will take on another form the moment the gamma rays strike it. The problem then arises, is that the electron, whose composition we wanted to study, does not remain in its original form. Werner Heisenberg called it the principle of uncertainty and said that an electron is not a substance and that it is difficult to find out its composition. The next question was to know about the medium to understand it. While looking for an answer to this problem, they realised that they did not know whether the basic element was a particle or a wave. Sometimes they look like particles and sometimes as waves and that this experience or feeling is real. It was realised that it looking like a particle or a wave depends on the process which had been used to find it. Hence, the experience of these minute elements depends on the observer and the process he applies. Although the scientist today is not aware of the innumerable atoms, yet uses them because he knows their nature.

Talking about this, Sir James Jeans says in his book *New Background of Science,* that for today's scientists, electrons, protons and photons are just like 'x', 'y', and 'z' of Algebra. What is happening today is that without knowing what these particles are, we use them and are able to conveniently make discoveries. As such, the scientific journey to find out about the universe has, in the words of Einstein, become, "to take out one obscure from another obscure."

2. In its journey to find out the basic element of the universe, science found that the particles or waves do not exist in isolation, but they move in a flow, which is a form of energy and that we interact with these energies. Earlier, light, temperature, magnetic force, electricity, sound, etc. were all considered to be different powers. However, with new discoveries, the process of unifying the powers started and four of these were considered to be the main forces.
   (i) **Gravitational power** – It is present within all main sub-atomic particles like electrons, protons, neutrons and nutrinos and is a force that controls the entire universe including the earth. However, no knowledge has, as yet, been gained on '*gravitone*' which is believed to be the cause of the gravitational pull.
   (ii) **Electro-magnetic force** – It has now been proved that temperature, electricity, sound, magnetism and all other powers are the electro-magnetic forces with varied wavelengths.
   (iii) **Strong Nuclear power** – It is the force that keeps the protons and the neutrons tied to the nucleus of the atom. This is one million times stronger than the electro-magnetic force.

(iv) **Weak Nuclear power** – Everything is included in these four powers. Weinberg and Abdus Salaam of Pakistan have unified the electro-magnetic and the strong and weak nuclear powers. However, the gravitational power has not been added on yet.

3. In his special theory of relativity, Einstein had unified matter and energy. He had said that matter is the broad expression of energy and through his famous equation **$E = mC^2$**, proved that both can be interconverted. Newton had said that space is uniform all around and time is linear. But, Einstein said that the universe was not a mere machine. Its activities are not mechanical. In fact, the universe is flexible and has various forms. Wherever there is an object and movement, space curves. Just as a fish swimming in water cuts through the water around it, similarly a star or a comet or a constellation brings about a change in the formation of time through which it passes.

   Space and time are not different because one does not exist without the other. Time has no identity of its own without incidents and one does not have any knowledge about incidents without time. This way, Einstein unified matter, energy, space and time.

   Thus, in short, the entire scientific journey of the west can be summerised like this. The entire world is made up of elements, elements are made up of atoms and atoms are made up of small particles. However, whether these particles are there or not is difficult to find out. Hence, they are all a flow and flow is a form of force or energy. This energy is of four kinds. The unification of three of these can be understood. They are in space (which is three dimensional) and space and time are not separate. Hence, the entire world is born out of the four-dimensional field of space and time. The unification of gravitational power has not been possible in this amalgamation. The day this happens, physics will probably end. The scientific journey of the west has come upto this.

The question that arises is suppose the gravitational power is also unified, then will the puzzle of the universe be solved? Will the ultimate truth about the world become known? It seems not, because then, some basic questions will arise. What is the human mind? What is intelligence? What are feelings? What is free will? What is its relationship with the broad world and the incidents that happen here? The most important, what is consciousness? Because till today, science has not taken the mind, consciousness, intelligence, etc. in its periphery and science is divided into categories like physics and biology, etc. A new kind of caste system seems to be coming up and this fragmented outlook is a major reason for this tragedy.

SCIENCE-JOURNEY OF INDIA

Since ancient times, we in India have contemplated some questions. What is the universe? How was it born? Why was it born? However, if these things were contemplated upon more contemplation was done on the human mind in which these questions arose.

The first medium of acquiring knowledge is the sense organs. Through these organs, a man can see, taste, smell, touch and hear and acquire knowledge. These are the media of the outer world. Various appliances increase the power of these organs.

Intuition was considered the second and the more important medium. Once the vibrations of the thoughts, feelings and desires are pacified, the body is used as a laboratory and the truth is revealed. These were the two media of acquiring knowledge and efforts were made to experience the inner feelings, and find the answers to the above questions. Although answers to the above questions are available in the *Vedas,* the *Brahmanas,* the *Upanishads,* the *Mahabharata,* the *Bhagwat* etc., but from the point of view of nuclear science, an anlysis of the universe was first established in a formulated way by Sage Kanaad, thousands of years ago, in his *Vaisheshik Darshan.*

On some issues, Sage Kanaad's philosophy goes much ahead of today's science. Sage Kanaad says that if a matter is made smaller, a time will come when it can not be made any smaller because if this is done, it will lose its old characteristics. The second thing he says is that matter has two states - molecular and mammoth. The molecular state is the minutest and this huge universe is mammoth. Moreover, the state of matter does not remain the same. Hence, Kanaad says:

> ***Dharma vishesh prasudaat dravya gun karma saamaanya vishesh samavaayanaam***
>
> ***Padaarthaanaam sadharmya vaidhamryaabhyaam tatvagyaana nihshreyasam.***
>
> – *(Vaisheshik Darshan –4)*

In Dharma, the salvation is achieved by the knowledge of the heterogeneity and the homogeinty of the collection of matter, properties, and work, ordinary and special.

What is matter? Sage Kanaad's interpretation of this is very extensive and amazing. He says –

Prithivyaapastejovaayuraakaasham Kaalodigaatma mana iti dravyaani.

– *(Vaisheshik Darshan 1/5)*

The earth, water, brilliance, air, sky, time, direction, living beings, the mind, etc. are all matter. Here some believe the earth, water, etc. to be our earth, water, etc. But it must, however, be kept in mind that these nine that have been named are the matter of the entire universe. Therefore, earth here does not mean the our world.

He says that the earth means the solid matter, water means the liquid form and air means the gaseous form. This was generally known to the world earlier too but Sage Kanaad says that brilliance is also matter, whereas in the 20th century, we have got the knowledge that matter and energy are one. Besides this, he also says that the sky is also matter and that the sky is without atom and all movement takes place with the assistance of the sky because there is a space or influence zone between the atoms. Hence we use words like *ghataakaash, mahaakaash and hridayaakaash* (Dark sky, massive sky and the sky of the heart or the mental canvas). Sage Kanaad says that space and time are also matter whereas in the west, this concept came up after the establishment of Einstein's Theory of Relativity.

According to Sage Kanaad, the mind and the spirit are also matter. Even modern science does not have the mentality to accept this concept.

Every matter is in the state of atom. They are dynamic and circular. Hence, Kanaad's *Sootra* are:

Nityam parimandalam.

– *(Vaisheshik Darshan 7/20)*

Atoms are small and big. In this connection Sage Kanaad says:

Eten deerghatwahriswatwe vyakhyaate.

– (Vaisheshik Darshan 7-1-17)

Attraction and repulsion are the cause for the atoms being big or small. Similarly, in the *Brahma Sutra,* it has been said that:

Mahad deerghavadva hriswaparimandalaabhyaam.

– (Brahmasutra 2-2-11)

This means small and big circles are made from the universe.

In reply to how atoms are influenced, sage Kanaad says:

Vibhavaanmahanaakaashastatha cha aatmaa.

– (Vaisheshik Darshan 7-22)

With the influence of the high energy, the sky and the spirit.

Speaking about how the process of creation takes place from atoms, Kanaad says through *paakaj* (the act of maturation). This act is also called *peelupaak* which means the atoms are assimilated through fire or heat. When two atoms meet, *dwayanuk* (couple of atoms) are created, with three, *trayanuk,* with four *chaturnuk* and this way all the broad things are created. They live for some time, then they decay and return to their original form.

Sage Kanaad considers the atom to be the final element. It is believed that when his life was ending, his disciples pleaded with him to take the name of God, but the only thing he said was *peelavah peelavah peelavah* which means *paramaanu paramaanu paramaanu.*

Sage Kapil went a little deeper and his *saankhya darshan* presents an extremely scientific definition of the universe. Sage Kapil said that anything which has an internal structure, it has varied forms. Hence, we cannot say anything about the shape of the thing with which this world is made up with certainly. All we can say is that they are very minute and that they have a special characteristic. Hence, he said that the world was *trigunaatmak* (made of three virtues) and these are *satgun, rajogun and tamogun.* Sage Kapil's commentary is amazing. He says that these three virtues are:

> ***Ladhvaadidharmah saadharmyam vaidharmyam cha gunaanaam.***
>
> – *(Saankhya Darshan 1-128)*

Equal because of the fact that they are minute, but from the point of virtue or properties, they are different. What is quality, virtue or attribute? He says–

> ***Preetyapreetivishaadaadyairgunaanaamanyoanyam Vaidhamryam.***
>
> – *(Saankhya Darshan 1-127)*

Attraction, repulsion and neutrality are the three attributes of these qualities. Their motion is because of attraction and repulsion. Hence, *Saankhya* says–

> ***Raagaviraagayoryogah srishtih***
>
> – *(Saankhya Darshan 2-9)*

The combination of attraction and repulsion is the creation. The entire universe is nothing but a game of attraction and repulsion. The power which makes all this happen is called operative power. All physical powers are amalgamated in this. But, who is this man who has the desire to know and in whose mind these questions arise, his mind and his apprehensions and where will they all finally integrate? The Vedanta has given a logical analysis and narrated the experience as per *saankhya*.

He said that before creation, nature was in an imperceptible situation but all virtues were in a state of equilibrium. This equilibrium gets broken by the determination of the basic element. The *Upanishads* have given a description of this –

Ekoaham bahusyaama

This determination is will-power. This breaks the equilibrium of the virtues and it gives rise to agitation in the imperceptible nature leading to the beginning of the process of creation. It first develops as a huge intelligence power. This is the power of knowledge. This starts the process of expressing the power of action in various forms. A basic power of knowledge is regulating everything - from a minute atom to the entire universe. This is proved by the following facts –

1. Amongst the great creations is the spiral symmetry of the galaxy. On the other hand, there is the double helix system of the minute genes.[1]
2. In his book entitled *Infinite is all Directions,* Freeman Dyson says, "From the point of form, an amazing equilibrium can be seen in the world. If we look at it in four contexts, it will become clear. (A) The entire scenario of the world, (B) Our earth, (C) Nucleus of an atom, and (d) Super string. Our earth is 10^{20} (1 followed by 20 zeros) times smaller than the

known universe. Compared with the earth, the shape of the nucleus of the atom is 10^{20} times smaller and the super string is 10^{20} times smaller than the nucleus of the atom.[2].

Saankhya says that the various things of the world and the various senses are made up of the ***panchatanmaatraa*** which is made up of the three *ahankaars (Vaikaari ahankaar; tejas ahankaar and bhootaadi ahankaar)* which comes from excellence. The wheel of creation keeps moving and in the same sequence, it ends at the time of annihilation or universal destruction. To tell us what the various powers are, how they keep the wheel of creation moving, how destruction takes place and all that is happening, *Vedanta Darshan* says – **Kampanaat.**

There is vibration and throbbing in creation and destruction. Lord Buddha says that the entire world is vibrating—***sabbopajjalito loko, sabbo loko pakampito.*** There is nothing solid in this world, only vibration.[3] Adi Shankaracharya says, "From an atom to the heavens and from ordinary power to spiritual power, there is vibration."[4] Even Swami Vivekanand says, "The entire world is vibration, throbbing. The only thing is that the mind has vigorous vibrations whereas the inanimates have weak vibrations. The creation and destruction of the universe is the result of these vibrations only. It is like the waves of the sea. Just as there is turmoil or vibrations above the sea, but below, it is peaceful, similarly, the basis of the world is Brahma and the tremors are only on the surface."

In this way, in the evaluation of the universe, he realised that the world and its creator have three levels—tangible which we can experience and feel when we are awake; intangible which we experience when we are asleep. The creation of both the worlds is different. The waking world is made up of physical atoms and the dream world is made up of emotional atoms. The measurement of time in the two is also different or we can say it is conditional. There is a third world also called the *Kaaran jagat* which we experience when we are in deep sleep.

As such, the different forms of the universe, the various powers and their creator were coordinated in the following way:

The **three worlds**—1. The tangible world, 2. Intangible world, and 3. *Kaaran jagat.*

The **three conditions or states**—1. *Jaagrit* or awakened, 2. *Swapna* (dream), and, 3. *Sushupti* (deep sleep).

The **three powers**—1. Action 2. Knowledge and 3. Desire.

The base from which all these three are created, has been called the *Brahma.* One can experience this in the fourth state, called the ***Tureeya*** state or state of unification.

There is immovable water deep inside the huge ocean, yet small and big waves keep rising and falling on its surface. In the same way, the entire universe keeps coming up like the waves and disappears like the ebbing waves in the massive *Brahma* Ocean. This has been called *Brahma,* the ultimate truth a description of which has been attempted in various forms in Indian literature.

Yato vaache nivartante apraapya manasaa saha

—(TU 12-4-1)

From where the voice comes back with the mind.

Yato va Imaani bhootaani jaayante yena jaataani jeevanti
Yena yat prayantbhisamvishanti tadvijigyaasasva cha tadbramheti.

– (TU 3-1-1)

Know from which all matter is born, lives and dies or is absorbed in. That is Brahma.

> ***Sa yatha urnanaabhih tantuna uchyaret yatha agneh Kshudraah vishphulingaah vyuccharanti evam eva asmaat aatmanah sarve praanaah sarve lokaah sarve devaah sarvaani bhootani vyuccharanti tasya Upanishad satyasya satyam iti praanaah vaee satyam teshaam eshah satyam.***
>
> – (*Brihadaaranyak Upanishad* 2-1-20)

This means the way the spider spins its web and the way sparks come out of fire, similarly all kinds of powers, all kinds of worlds, all kinds of gods and the entire tangible world is born out of the soul. Know the soul; go near it, it is the truth of the truths. Basic energy is the truth, but the soul is the truth of this also.

Thus, in the opinion of the Indian intelligence, the universe is the momentary expression of the massive ocean of consiousness. Many western scientists have also contemplated on this subject. J.W.N. Sulivan's interview with Max Planck was published in the *Observer*, dated January 25, 1931. In this, Sullivan asks whether consciousness can be explained under matter and its rules? In reply, Max Planck said, "I don't think so. In my opinion, consciousness is original and matter is the result of this. Matter is nothing but an extension of consciousness."[5]

Swami Vivekanand has expressed it thus. He says, "It seems that the flow of consciousness emits from the interior and is flowing incessantly towards the physical world."

There can be no absolute demarcation between the living and the non-living because there is unity and solidarity in the world. On May 10, 1901, Jagdish Chandra Basu had, through experiments, proved this before the scientists of the world at the Royal Institute[6]. When a dose of caustic potash, which creates poison, was put on a piece of tin, its electric pulsation or throbbing stopped just as it does in a living cell. Similarly, when an antidote to the poison was injected, the metal was regenerated. After giving many demonstrations to this effect and by presenting self-acquired records of proof, Bose finished his speech in the following words –

"In view of such natural facts, can we draw a boundary line between physical reaction and the action and reaction on the body? There is no such boundary line."

"When I saw the mute testimonies of records and the granule or particle that trembles in the waves of light, life of our earth and the shining sun and scanned the unity existing in all things, it was then that I was somewhat able to understand the message that my ancestors had announced about three thousand years ago on the banks of the river Ganga. They had said that in all the changing forms of this world, there is only one truth, only one - and nothing else."[7]

THE MEANS TO KNOW THE ULTIMATE TRUTH

Once, Heisenberg, the father of the theory of uncertainty asked Neils Bohr, the great scientist who enunciated the planetary model of the atom, "If the internal formation of the atom is as indescribable as you are saying and that we do not have words to express it, then how can we hope to ever be able to understand it?" At this, Neils Bohr became quiet for some time. Then, hesitatingly, he said, "We can understand even after all this, but we will first have to learn the meaning of understanding."[8] There is depth in what Bohr said. One is reminded of a statement by Einstein in the context of how this understanding could come about.

Someone asked Einstein how can one know the ultimate reality of the world. Einstein said, "The appliances (senses and intelligence) we use to try and understand the world, are a part of this world only. They also fall under the periphery of space, time and cause relation whereas truth is beyond this periphery." Hence, he said, "Jump above your own mind", but how they have to jump, the west does not know. Our *yoga sadhana* and various other forms of *sadhana* have expounded ways to reach the timeless state which is outside the periphery of country, time and cause relation.

The *Shwetaashwar Upanishad* describes what the world is. What is the reason for its existance. While analyzing it, some considered time to be the reason, some considered nature to be the cause, some said it was sudden coincidence, some said nature, some a collection of matter, some considered man to be the cause and someone thought it was a collection of all these. But what will happen when we do not find the ultimate truth? In reply, the *Upanishad* says –

> ***The dhyaanayogaanugataa apashyan***
> ***Devaatmshaktim swagunaeernigoodhaam.***
> ***Yah kaaranaani mikhilaani taani***
> ***Kaalaatmayuktaanyadhitishthatyeka.***
>
> – *(Shwetaashwar Upanishad 1 – 3)*

This means that when this happened, he took the shelter of *dhyaan* (meditation) and *yoga,* and going into the internal depths, perceived the supreme power that is the cause of this entire world including time.

And when this perception occurs, we understand that all that is known and unknown is the expression of that one alone and that the entire world, its powers, animals, birds, insects, moths, trees, humans are all various forms of that one element. This experience gives rise to integral vision. This is one of the best gifts from India which ends the differences between the living and the non-living and solves all the problems of the world and its biggest mystery, that is man. Only India can give this knowledge to the world.

THE SCIENTIFIC OUTLOOK OF THE WEST AND ITS CONSEQUENCES

The history of the scientific development in the west had a major role to play in its scientific outlook.

1. The process of scientific development in the West had to suffer the organised cruel assaults of the church. As such, science there has been a little more inclined towards materialism.
2. Because of the thinking of Bacon and Descartes, only those things that were proven through mathematical interpretations and experiments were considered true. As such, all other aspects of life, whether they were psychology, art or literature, were all kept out of the periphery of science. A concept was formed that the human mind, his feelings, his family were not within the periphery of science. They believed that matter and mind are two separate things and that only matter is a subject of science and that anyone who tries to link the mind with matter, is unscientific.
3. Newton presented the concept of a mechanical universe according to which, this world is a machine. If one can acquire knowledge about each part of the machine, then one can get control over the machine. From the view of gaining control, the mentality to win the nature was born. As a result, the earlier concept of looking at nature as a mother was replaced by the concept that it was to be enjoyed and the mentality to use our scientific capabilities to torment nature, to exploit it and to gather things of comfort

for ourselves was developed. This is the cause of many of todays problems.

4. Newton's concept of a mechanical universe, which means that everything works as per set rules, was applied by Darwin in the field of biology, by John Lock in the field of sociology, by Marx in the field of the process of social change and Malthus in the field of economics from which developed an inanimate but hard system.
5. The principles of quantum theory and relativity destroyed the concepts of a mechanical universe, certainty or definiteness and some fundamental or basic particles because a number of energised electrons, hydrones, meons, mesons, etc. inside an atom are striking against each other and making new energies. Hence, one can definitely not say what is happening in the atom right now. We can only express what is happening by saying that such and such a thing may possibly be happening.

Hence, today's scientist is also compelled to use the same words that the Indian philosophers in the ancient times used for that ultimate truth. For example, Oppenheimer said, "If anyone asks me if atoms of energy are stationary then I will say no. If anyone asks me if they are moving, I will say no. If anyone asks me if they are a form of particles, I will say no. If anyone asks me if they are waves, I will say no. If anyone says if they are neither this nor that, then what are they, then I will say it is just like that." On this, we are reminded of the *Eishawaasya Upanishad* in which the sage says:

Tadejati tannejati tad doore tadwantike
Tadantarasya sarvaswa tadu sarvasyasya baahyatah
ishavaasya –5

It moves, it does not move, it is far, it is near, it is within everyone, it is outside everyone.

Similarly, today's science says that there is duality in the entire world. There is matter and anti-matter. If one atom of energy in the universe is moving clockwise and moving upwards, then side by side, somewhere else, it's counterpart is moving anti-clockwise and moving downwards. Indian philosophers had also said much earlier that the world is full of dualities – dualities between man and nature, joys and sorrows, cold and heat, day and night.

Science today says that everything in the world is interrelated. To explain this, they use words from physics and say. 'Inseparable quantum interconnectedness where every particle contains every other particle.' Indian sages had expressed this in very simple terms by saying that the seed comes from the tree and the tree comes from the seed. ***Yadpinde tad brahmaande*** which means that whatever is in the body, is in the universe too.

This way, with the development of science, scientists in the west have started thinking that truth cannot be discovered on physical ground alone. Hence, scientists like Heisenberg, Irwin Schrodinger, James Jeanes, Fridzofkapra, Gezhukov, Geofriechwe etc. believe that if one wants to understand the world, one must understand the mind and the conscience. Thus, one will have to contemplate this not in parts, but in an integrated way. So, today, people are talking about a **holistic approach.** The basic question, however is that even today, this outlook is not as influential as it ought to have been. Even today, science is divided into groups. Physics, biology and psychology are all working in their own fields. There is a lack of a holistic outlook. As a result, alongwith scientific development, man is standing at the crossroad between human pleasure and problems.

6. Einstein had said that science could denature platinum but it is unable to denature evil from human mind. Hence, while science has, on one hand thrown man into the sea of comfort to swim, it has, on the other hand posed a great danger for the very existance of mankind.

TODAY'S TRAGEDY

Science has, today, helped man go into space, set foot on the moon and return, scan the mineral resources hidden in the womb of the earth on his screen and made it possible to scan the minute fibres or tendrils of the brain. Today, anyone can go around the whole earth in 24 hours and can send his message from one end of the world to another within a second and sitting in the comfort of his drawing room, he can see all that is happening around the world on his TV screen and this progress has been very fast. These are the creative aspects of science.

On the other hand, man has lost the feeling of motherhood that he had towards nature. That has been replaced by a feeling that it has to be enjoyed. It is because of this that science is becoming an enemy of the entire living creation. While on one hand, radiations from the factories are becoming the cause for many deadly diseases, depletion of the ozone layer, which protects the earth from the ultra-violet rays of the sun, is also endangering the earth. Jungles have been cut down. As a result, climate is becoming irregular. The temperature of the earth is rising because of uncontrolled industrialisation. The recently held Earth Summit warned that if the temperature of the world rises by 2.5 or 3 degrees, then the glaciers will melt, the level of sea water will rise by 80 cm and many cities and islands will be drowned. Sound pollution is increasing so much that it will take us close to madness. Industrial waste is polluting water. Animals are cruelly or mercilessly killed for our own pleasure. So, the plants, animals and the entire living world is in danger.

A long time ago, Bertrand Russell had written in his book *Science and Its Impact on Society* that "Man today is living between human skill and human folly. If his prudence does not increase alongwith his skill, then the more and more development will end in more and more sorrow."

An incident easily describes this situation. The Development Council of India had a conference in Ahmedabad. A Jain ascetic, who had come there, narrated his experience. Once, there was a programme at a University, where a speaker said that science thinks about a problem that is going to come up or occur 100 years from now. For example, since one knows that coal will finish in the next 100 years, science is looking for an alternative source of energy today. At this, the Jain ascetic said that the way scientific development does not follow any principles, is valueless and is becoming an enemy of creation, the manner in which chemical and annihilatory atomic weapons are being made and the way in which man is becoming selfish and greedy, the time is not far when this ability of science will change the whole world into coal. Hence, there is need to deliberate on who will burn this coal in the world turned into coal itself.

TODAY'S NEED

Swami Ranganathanandaji, the Chief of the Rama Krishna Mission, has made a statement that is worthy of contemplation. The main question is whether science is ready to cross its limited materialist boundary to discover truth? Will the search for truth still be made by keeping aside human consciousness and human mind? Is life only a particle? Is life a mere coincidence of DNA and RNA or is it some other deep valuable thing? Do we today, have enough courage to accept that abstract or intangible element or that *satyasya satya* (truth of truth) as ultimate truth? The completeness of our search of truth and the future of human beings depends on the answer to this question. As Prof. Fritzofkapra says, modern physicists experience the world with an extremely logical brain and experiments whereas a spiritualist experiences it with a logical brain and realizations. Both investigate in different ways and reach conclusions. They will either join together later or break up or depreciate. However, for the complete knowledge of the world they are both necessary and complementary to each other. A Chinese philosopher has said that a spiritualist knows the root of Tao (a name well known for the ultimate truth or god in China) but he does not know the branches, whereas a scientist knows the branches of Tao but does not know the root. A spiritualist does not feel the need for a scientist and a scientist does not feel the need for a spiritualist. Man, however, needs both.

INDIAN SCIENTIFIC OUTLOOK AND ITS RELEVANCE

1. Only one truth spreads throughout the world. This has not only been proved by reason or argument or on intellectual level, but by actual perception attained by moving outside the periphery of country, time and reason with the help of meditation. This experience develops an integrated outlook which thinks of the human being, society and nature as a whole and not in parts. They experienced that whatever we do, it influences the entire environment. Hence, development here was in coordination with society, environment and nature.
2. Since ancient times, it has been said that to acquire complete knowledge, knowledge of the world and

of one who knows the world is required and in order to get complete knowledge of the basis of the world, both physical and spiritual knowledge is required. The same thing has been expressed in various books. In the *Gita,* it has been said that to acquire completeness, knowledge of the *kshetra* (that is the entire world) and *kshetragya* (that is one who knows that world) is necessary. It was expounded in this manner. The *Upanishads* said, one must have knowledge of *para* (that is the main element, of which all this has been born) and *apara* (the extension of the main element that is this world). The Shankaraacharya called this as *Vastu Tantra,* i.e. entire universe and *Drashta,* i.e. the observer of this universe and said that knowledge about both of these should be acquired. Hence, according to Indian tradition, materialism is not in opposition or contrary to spiritualism but it is its broad manifestation.

3. Because of having one outlook towards the entire world, the activities of life, the thinking and behaviour has been one of coordination, cooperation and complementary, whose manifestation can be seen in ordinary life too.
4. Just as the *vaidya* in Ayurveda prays before plucking a herb for treatment saying that the plant has life but since it is required for the protection of a human life, therefore he is plucking it. Hence, he plucks only as much as is required.
   - Even an uneducated and illiterate grandmother stops her grandchild from shaking a tree in the evening saying that the tree is sleeping.
   - Everything in this world is godly or divine. Hence it should be used with restraint. This advice has come out of this vision of oneness.

- In the *Shantimantra* (the chant for peace), prayers have been given for the welfare of all nature by saying that there should be peace in the *dyao* (heaven), *antariksh* (space), *prithvi* (earth), water, medicines, herbs and the gods of the world.
- Because of maternal feelings towards nature, the cow, the river and the tree, etc. were all considered worthy of worship and materialistic development did not become the opponent of nature or creation.
- While giving the various destructive powers, the person, his character and his nature were all taken into consideration.

Thus, the key for the amalgamation of science and spiritualism for humanity which is standing at the crossroads is with India and it has to play its role in the future. A few years ago, Arnold Toyanby, the Nobel Prize winner and famous scholar of history from England had, at the convocation of Edinburgh, said, "India will be the leader in the 21st century. India will make great progress in every field and what is more, will harmonise science and religion, the only country that could and would do it."

OUR RESPONSIBILITY

Scientists, thinkers, historians and wise men from all over the world are looking hopefully towards India. For the fulfillment of this task, it is necessary to take India once again to the height of glory. To build such an India, the development of science, technology and arts and crafts will have to be taken to great heights. Since independence and till recent times, just a glimpse of it has been seen. When Jagdish Chandra Basu proved the oneness of the living and the non-living, when the world acknowledged the mathematical genius of Ramanujan, when, based on the behaviour of the photon particles and Satyendranath Bose' commentary on it, such particles were named 'Boson', Einstein was so impressed by his research papers that he added his name to it and insisted that it be called Bose-Einstein Statistics and not Einstein-Bose Statistics. Acharya P.C. Rai laid the foundation for the chemical industry in India, Chandrashekhar Venkataraman was awarded the Nobel Prize for the Raman Effect related to light, the measurement of the life and death of stars carried out by Chandrashekhar, is known throughout the world as Chandrashekhar Limit, Homi Jahangir Bhabha did not only lay the foundation of atomic science, he also laid the foundation of the first nuclear reactor when America refused to co-operate with India in the setting up a nuclear reactor. The world was astonished at his imagination to make the *sanlayan* process which generates energy in the stars, possible on earth.

While Vikram Sarabhai laid the foundation of the space programme, Dr. Abdul Kalaam, the present President of India, strengthened the country's safety by making a series of missiles - **Prithvi, Naag, Aakash, Trishul, Agni I and II**. After America's refusal to provide the technology, Vijay Bhatkar made the super computer with indigenous technology. Our scientists succeeded in making atomic energy for the Tarapur nuclear power station. They also succeeded in making the cryogenic engine with indigenous technology and sending up satellites at a distance of 36,000 kms with the help of our very own rocket, the GSLV. We are moving ahead in the manufacture of a super conductor too.

Even after all these achievements, a technique, which will make the progress or development of science concordant with nature, that will not pollute the environment and is for the welfare of entire world, can be possible only with India's integrated scientific outlook. While keeping a sense of respect for the present scientists who are trying to develop such a technique, we will also have to develop a sense of pride in our ancestors and their achievements, their thoughts and knowledge, so that the present generation can take that ancient integrated scientific tradition forward, to be a guiding light for the entire world. This work is waiting for the manliness of present generation. As Sir Jagdish Chandra Basu, the great scientist of modern India wrote in the foreword of one of his books:[9]

> To my countrymen
> Who will yet claim
> The intellectual heritage
> of their ancestors.

It is only with the valour of present generation that we will be able to take our country on the path to ultimate glory or all round progress and it will succeed in playing its role decided by destiny for the welfare of humanity. May God give us the determination, inspiration and capability for this great task.

□

References (Chapterwise)

CHAPTER-1

1. Surendranath Gupt, *Sone ki Chidiya Lutere Angrez*, p. 10.
2. Samuel Huntington, *The Clash of Civilisations*, p. 86.
3. Dr. Murli Manohar Joshi, *Vibha*, p. 17.
4. Abdul Kalaam, *India 2020*, pp. 27-28.
5. Dr. Murli Manohar Joshi, *The State of Science and Technology in India*, p. 8.
6. Dr. Joshi, *Vibha*.

CHAPTER-2

1. Swami Ranganathanandaji, *Parivartansheel Samaaj ke liye Shashwat Mulya*, p. 194.
2. Dr. Murli Manohar Joshi, *The State of Science and Technology in India*, p. 13.
3. Dr. Murli Manohar Joshi, *The State of Science and Technology in India*, p. 9-10 and P.C. Roy, *A History of Hindu Chemistry*,V2, p. viii.
4. Dr. Satya Prakash, *Vaigyaanik Vikaas ki Bharatiya Parampara*, p. 175 and P.C. Roy, *A History of Hindu Chemistry*, V2, p. vii.

CHAPTER-3

1. Carl Pearson, *Grammar of Science 1900*, p. 6.
2. Gurudatt, *Vigyan aur Vigyan*, p. 12.
3. Rao Saheb Vajhe, *Hindi Shilp Shastra*, p. 8-9.

CHAPTER-4

1. Rao Saheb Vajhe, *Pracheen Hindi Shilp Shastra Saar*, p. 136.
2. Tadaiv, p. 136.
3. Tadaiv, p. 136.
4. Tadaiv, pp. 138-139.
5. P.P. Holey, *Machines in Sanskrit Literature*, p. 35.

CHAPTER-5

1. N.G. Dongre, *The Physics*, pp. 27-28.
2. Tadaiv, p. 30.
3. Bhaskaracharya, *Siddhant Shiromani*, p. 477.
4. N.G. Dongre, *The Physics*, p. 24.
5. Tadaiv, p. 26.
6. Tadaiv, p. 30.
7. Anantacharya Indological Research Institute, Bombay, Series No. XV, February, 1983, p. 28.

CHAPTER-6

1. Paatheya Kan, *Bharatiya Vigyan Visheshank*, p. 33.
2. *The Week*, June 24, 2001.
3. Dharmapal, *Indian Science and Technology in the Eighteenth Century*, p. 211.
4. *Tadaiv*, pp. 220-222, 235.
5. *Tadaiv*, p. 238.
6. *Tadaiv*, p. 248.
7. Vigyan Bharati, *Science and Technology in Ancient India*, pp. 76-77.

CHAPTER-7

1. Subraiyya Shastri, Maharshi Bharadwaj, *Vaimanik Shastra,* p. 2.
2. *Tadaiv,* p. 3.
3. *Tadaiv,* p. 4.
4. *Tadaiv,* p. 12.
5. *Tadaiv,* p. 16.
6. *Tadaiv,* p. 42.
7. *Tadiav,* p. 115.
8. M.P. Rao, *Vaimanik Shastra, Rediscovered* – Appendix D.
9. *Tadaiv,* Appendix E.
10. *Tadiav,* Appendix F.

CHAPTER-8

1. Bhikshu Chamanlal, *Hindu America,* p. 359.
2. Kalyan, *Hindu Sanskriti Ank–1950,* p. 734.
3. *Tadaiv,* p. 734.
4. Udayan Indurkar, *Drishtakala Sadhak,* p. 32.
5. Kalyan, *Hindu Sanskriti Ank–1950,* p. 735.

CHAPTER-9

1. Shilp Sanshodhan Pratishthan, Nagpur, *Dacca Muslin,* p. 5.
   For more information, see *Dacca Muslin – Modern Review,* July 1911.

CHAPTER-10

1. Bharti Krishna Teerthji, *Vaidic Ganit,* p. xviii.
2. Gunakar Mule, *Arya Bhatta,* p. 43.

CHAPTER-11

1. Vasudev Potdar, *Kaalyatra,* p. 14.
2. Dr. Ravi Prakash Arya, *Bharatiya Kaalganana ka Vaigyanik va Vaishwik Swaroop,* p. 8.

3. *Tadaiv*, pp. 10-11.
4. *Tadaiv*, pp. 12-13.
5. *Tadaiv*, p. 14.
6. *Tadaiv*, p. 21.
7. *Tadaiv*, p. 25.
8. *Tadaiv*, p. 44.
9. *Tadaiv*, p. 45.
10. *Tadaiv*, p. 48.
11. Carl Sagan, *Cosmos*, p. 214.
12. Arthur C. Clarke, *Men and Space*, p. 166.
13. Dr. B.B. Naik, *Vigyan Adhyatmana Maarge*, p. 40.

CHAPTER-12

1. Gunakar Mule, *Bhaskaracharya*, p. 80.
2. Dharmapal, *Indian Science and Technology in the Eighteenth Century*, p. 48.
3. Rigveda, *Sayan Bhashya*, 1–71–9, 1–50–9.
4. Bhaskaracharya, *Siddhanta Shiromani*, p. 344.
5. *Tadaiv*, p. 346.
6. Gunakar Mule, *Arya Bhatta*, p. 66.
7. Ramnivasrai, *Aryabhattiya*, p. 106.
8. *Shrimad Bhagwat Gita*, Gita Press, p. 249.

CHAPTER-13

1. Rao Saheb Vajhe, *Prachin Hindi Shilp Shastra Saar*, p. 32.
2. Vigyan Bharati, *Science and Technology in Ancient India*, p. 16.
3. *Tadaiv*, p. 17.
4. *Shilp Sanshodhan Pratishthan*, Nagpur, p. 12.
5. *Tadaiv*, p. 12.
6. *Tadaiv*, p. 13.
7. *Tadaiv*, p. 7.
8. *Tadaiv*, pp. 7-8.

9. Kalyan, *Hindu Sanskriti Ank*–1950, p. 674.
10. *Shilp Sanshodhan Pratishthan,* Nagpur, p. 12.

CHAPTER-14

1. *Science and Technology in Ancient India,* p. 34.
2. Paatheya Kan, *Bharatiya Vigyan Visheshank,* p. 34.
3. P.C. Roy, *A History of Hindu Chemistry*—vi, p. xxv.
4. *Tadaiv,* p. xxiv.
5. *Tadaiv*–V1, Sanskrit Text, p. 15.
6. *Tadaiv*–V2, Sanskrit Text, p. 4.
7. *Tadaiv*–V1, Sanskrit Text, p. 14.
8. Prof. A.R. Vasudev, *Indian Tradition of Chemistry and Chemical Technology.*
9. P.C. Rai, *A History of Hindu Chemistry*–V2, Sanskrit Text, p. 79.

CHAPTER-15

1. *Mahabharata, Shanti Parva,* 184th Chapter, Shloka 9-17.
2. Dr. Anupama Devpujari, *Botany in Sanskrit Literature,* Classification by Charak.
3. *Tadaiv*
4. Brajendra Nath Seel, *The Positive Sciences of the Ancient Hindus,* p. 173.
5. Dr. Nityendra Nath Sarkar, *An Introduction to the Vriksha Ayurveda of Parashar.*
6. *Tadaiv.*
7. Dr. Vidyadhar Sharma 'Guleri', *Sanskrit mein Vigyan,* p. 52.
8. *Tadaiv,* p. 53.
9. *Tadaiv,* p. 54.
10. *Mahabharata, Shanti Parva,* 184th chapter—Shloka 16.
11. Dr. Vidyadhar Sharma 'Guleri', *Sanskrit mein Vigyan,* p. 57.
12. *Tadaiv,* p. 58.

13. Divakar Sen, Ajay Kumar Chakravarty—*J.C. Bose Speaks*, pp. 204-205.

CHAPTER-16

1. Dr. Vidyadhar Sharma 'Guleri', *Sanskrit mein Vigyan*, p. 143.
2. *Tadaiv*, p. 143.
3. *Tadaiv*, p. 144.
4. Girija Prasanna Majumdar and Suresh Chandra Banerjee, *Krishi Parashar*, p. 6.
5. Dharmapal, *Indian Science and Technology in the Eighteenth Century*, p. 180.
6. *Tadaiv*, p. 203.
7. *Tadaiv*, p. 180.

CHAPTER-17

1. Dr. Vidyadhar Sharma 'Guleri', *Sanskrit mein Vigyan*, p. 134.
2. *Tadaiv*, pp. 134-137.

CHAPTER-18

1. Dr. Nagaratna and G.R. Nagendra, *Integrated Approach of Yoga Therapy for Positive Health.*
2. Dr. Vidyadhar Sharma 'Guleri', *Sanskrit mein Vigyan*, p. 99.
3. *Sanskrit Vigyan Vaibhavam*, p. 14.
4. *Tadaiv*, p. 10.
5. Dr. Vidyadhar Sharma 'Guleri', *Sanskrit mein Vigyan*, pp. 101-102.
6. *Tadaiv*, p. 103.
7. *Tadaiv*, p. 100.
8. Paatheya Kan, *Bharatiya Vigyan Visheshank*, pp. 61-62.
9. *Tadaiv*, p. 64.

10. *Tadaiv*, pp. 65-66.
11. Dr. Murli Manohar Joshi, *Bharatvarsh mein Vigyan va Praudyogiki ki Sthiti*, pp. 14-15.
12. *Vigyan Bharati Pradeepika*, Ank 8–Number 1-2002, pp. 89, 113.

CHAPTER-19

1. Dr. Pradeep Kumar Dixit, *Sangeet Martand* Pt. Onkar Nath Thakur, p. 17.
2. Brajendra Nath Seel, *The Positive Sciences of the Ancient Hindus*, p. 159.
3. *Tadaiv*, p. 161.
4. *Tadaiv*, p. 163.

CHAPTER-20

1. L.S. Wakankar, Ganeshavidya, English, p. 3.
2. Dr. Murli Manohar Joshi, *Pragya Pravaah*, pp. 65-68.

CHAPTER-21

1. Vasudev Potdar, *Kaalyatra*, p. 175.
2. *Tadaiv*, p. 176.
3. Satyanarain Goenka, *Nirmal Dhara Dharm Ki*, p. 107.
4. Brajendra Nath Seel, *The Positive Sciences of Ancient Hindus*, p. 122.
5. Swami Jitatmanand, *Modern Physics and Vedanta*, p. 36.
6. Vishwa Priya Mukherji, *Jagdish Chandra Bose*, p. 43.
7. *Tadaiv*, pp. 43-44.
8. *Tadaiv*, pp. 38, 39.
9. Divakar Sen, Ajay Kumar Chakravarty—*J.C. Bose Speaks*, p. 209.

□

References (Books)

HINDI

1. *Vigyan aur Vigyan*—Gurudatt—Shashwat Sanskrit Parishad, New Delhi-1972
2. *Bharatiya Kaal Ganana*—Dr. Ravi Prakash Arya—Akhil Bharatiya Itihas Sankalan Yojana,New Delhi
3. *Bhaskaracharya*—Gunakar Mule—Gyan Vigyan Prakashan, New Delhi-1995
4. *Arya Bhatta*—Gunakar Mule—Gyan Vigyan Prakashan, New Delhi-1999
5. *Arya Bhatt*—G Gyananand—Bharat Bharati Bal Pustak Mala, Nagpur-1997
6. *Sone Ki Chidiya aur Lutere Angrez*—Surendranath Gupt—Granth Academy, New Delhi-1996
7. *Hindi Vaisheshik Darshan Prashastpad Bhashya*—Pt. Dhundiraj Shastri—Chaukhamba Sanskrit Sansthan, Varanasi-1998
8. *Bharatvarsh mein Vigyan va Praudyogiki ki Sthiti*—Dr. Murli Manohar Joshi—R.S. Chitlangia Foundation, Kolkata
9. *Aryabhattiya*—Ramniwas Rai—Indian National Science Academy, New Delhi-1976
10. *Sanskrit mein Vigyan*—Dr. Vidyadhar Sharma 'Guleri'—Sanskrit Bharati, New Delhi-2000

11. *Vaisheshik Darshan—Ek Adhyayan*—Shri Narayan Mishra—Chaukhamba Sanskrit Series, Varanasi-1968
12. *Agyat ki Ore*—Parmanand Patel—Bharatiya Vidya Bhawan, Mumbai-1982
13. *Niramay*—Dr. Govind hari Marathe, Gwalior
14. *Vishwa ki Kaal Yatra*—Vasudev Potdar—Akhil Bharatiya Itihaas Sankalan Yojana, New Delhi-2000
15. *Pracheen Bharat Mein Vigyan evam Praudyogiki*—Sankalan—Vigyan Bharati, Mumbai-2002
16. *Vaidic Ganit*—Jagatguru Swami Shri Bharati Krishna Teertha ji—Motilal Banarasidas, New Delhi-1996
17. *Vaidic Ganit Nirdeshika*—Sankalan—Vidya Bharati, Kurukshetra-2000
18. *Hindu Sanskriti Ank* (Kalyan)—Sankalan—Gita Press, Gorakhpur-1950
19. *Mahabharata* (Shanti Parv) —Maharshi Vyas—Gita Press, Gorakhpur
20. *Shrimad Bhagwat*—Maharshi Vyas—Gita Press, Gorakhpur
21. *Brihadaaranyak Upanishad*—Gita Press, Gorakhpur
22. *Sanskrit Vigyan Vaibhavam*—Sankalan—Rashtriya Sanskrit Vidyapeeth, Tirupati-2000
23. *Taitareeya Upanishad*—Gita Press, Gorakhpur
24. *Shwetaashwar Upanishad*—Gita Press, Gorakhpur
25. *Saankhya Darshan*
26. *Pragya Pravaah*—Dr. Murli Manohar Joshi—Parag Prakashan, Delhi-1991
27. *Drishta Kala Sadhak*—Udayan Indurkar—Prakashan Vibhag Sanskar Bharati, Agra-2003
28. *Nirmal Dhara Dharm Ki*—Satyanarain Goenka—Vipashyana Vishodhan Nyas, Igatpuri, Distt. Nashik-2000
29. *Jagdish Chandra Bose*—Vishwa Priya Mukherji—

Prakashan Vibhag – Ministry of Information and Broadcasting-1993

ENGLISH

1. *Art the Interface* – Dr. C.G. Ramachandra Nair - Swadeshi Science Movement, Kerala-2000
2. *The Tao of Physics* – Fritjof Capra – Flamingo – London-1983
3. *The Turning Point* – Fritjof Capra – Flamingo – London-1985
4. *J.C. Bose Speaks* – Editor – Dibakar Sen – Puthipatra, Kolkata – 1985
5. *The Positive Science of the Ancient Hindus* – Brajendra Nath Seel, Motilal Banarasidass, Delhi-1985
6. *Indian Science and Technology in the Eighteenth Century* – Dharmapal – India Press-2000
7. *Modern Physics and Vedanta* – Swami Jitatmananda – Bharatiya Vidya Bhawan-1986
8. *Science, Ethics and Holistic Values*-Swami Jitatmananda – Bharatiya Vidya Bhawan-1986
9. *Hindu America* – Chaman Lal – V.V. Research Institute-1956
10. *Botany in Sanskrit Literature* – Dr. Anupama Devpujari – Sanskrit Bharati, New Delhi-2000
11. *The Physics* – Dr. N.G. Dongre – Sanskrit Bharati, New Delhi-2000
12. *Metallurgy in Sanskrit Literature* – Dr. V.K. Didolkar – Sanskrit Bharati, New Delhi-2000
13. *Machines in Sanskrit Literature* – P.P. Holay – Sanskrit Bharati, New Delhi-2000
14. *Indian Tradition of Chemistry and Chemical Technology* – Prof. A.R. Vasudeva Murthy – Sanskrit Bharati, New Delhi-2000
15. *Medicine and Surgery in Ancient India* – K.H. Krishna

Murthy — Sanskrit Bharati, New Delhi-2000
16. *Cosmos* — Carl Sagan, Ballantine Books — New York-1980
17. *Man and Space* — Arthur C. Clarke — Life Science Library-1965
18. *A History of Hindu Chemistry* — P.C. Roy — Shaibya Prakashan Bilenay, Kolkata — 9th Centenary Edition-2002
19. *Karsi Parasarn* — Girija Prasanna Majumdar and Suresh Chandra Banerjee — The Asiatic Society — Kolkata — May-2001
20. *Integrated Approach of Yoga Therapy for Positive Health* — Dr. Nagarathana and H.R. Naghdra — Vivekanand Yoga Anusandhan Kendra, Bangalore

SANSKRIT

1. *Vaimanik Shastra — Maharshi Bharadwaj* — Subraiyya Shastri — G.R. Jyosar — Mysore
2. *Sanskrit Vigyan Vaibhavam* — Rashtriya Sanskrit Vidyapeeth, Tirupati-2000
3. *Siddhanta Shiromani* — Bhaskaracharya — Sampoornanand University, Varanasi-1981
4. *Bharatasya Vigyan Parampara* — Sankalan — Sanskrit Bharati, New Delhi-2001

MARATHI

1. *Hindi Shilp Shastra* — Part I — Krishnaji Vinayak Vajhe — Dhondo Krishna Sathe — Pune-1928
2. *Ganesh Vidya* — Scribe L.S. Wakankar — Maan Sammaan Prakashan — Pune-1998

GUJARATI

1. *Vigyan Adhyatm Na Marge* — Dr. B.G. Naik, Life Mission Trust — Vadodara-1997

2. *Bas Isi Disha Se Pratham Prakash Hua Tha*—Natu Bhai Thakkar—Rashtra Chetna Prakashan—Ahmedabad-2001

VARIOUS RESEARCHES AND SOUVENIRS

1. *Vaimanika Shastra Rediscovered*—A Project Study—Wg. Cdr. M.P. Rao (Retd), Bangalore-2001
2. The Study of Various Materials Described in Ansabodhini of Maharshi Bharadwaja—N.G. Dongre, Prof. P. Ramachandra Rao—F.W.A. National Metallurgical Laboratory, Jamshedpur-1999
3. Swadeshi Praan Vigyan Rashtriya Sangoshthi—Sankshipt Prativedan, Jabalpur-1992
4. *Shilp Sanshodhan Pratishthan*, Nagpur—Editor-R.M. Pujari
5. *Vibha*—Vigyan Bharati Smarika - Vigyan Aur Sanskrit, Gwalior-1999
6. *Vigyan Bharati Pradeepika*—Edition 8, Number-1-2002
7. *Paatheya Kan*—Bharatiya Vigyan Visheshank, Jaipur, November-2001
8. An Introduction to the Vriksha Ayurveda of Parasara, Nitendra Nath Sircar—*Journal of the Royal Asiatic Society of Bengali Letters* V, XVI—No. 1-1950
9. Anantaarcha Indological Research Institute—Mumbai—Series No. XV—February 1983.

□□□